# STEPHEN BIESTY'S

# ANCIENT WORLD

## Egypt • Rome • Greece
### in spectacular cross-section

OXFORD
UNIVERSITY PRESS

# Contents

## EGYPT

## ROME

# GREECE

# EGYPT

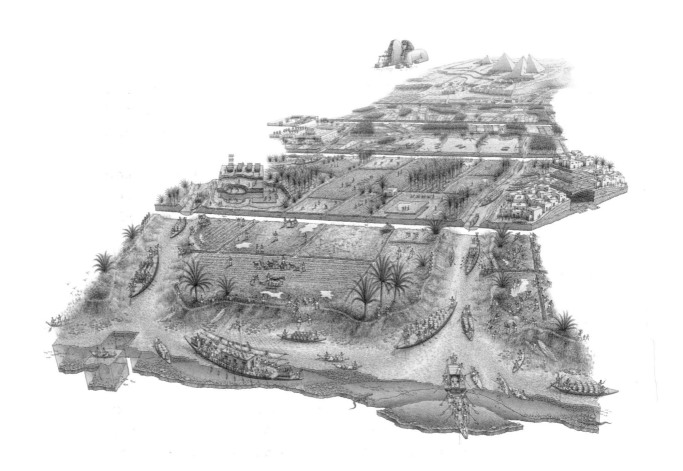

# 'My Land' by Dedia, son of Wennufer

Dedia's family house

Wennufer

Mutnofret, Dedia's mother

Dedia

Aunt Meritat

Ipuia

In the beginning Atum the Sun god created himself. Later came Nut and Geb, the Heaven and the Earth. And at the centre of the Earth appeared Egypt, the Kingdom of the Two Crowns. It has existed longer than anyone can remember.

This is my land. Watched over by the many gods and goddesses, it is the finest place in all the world. I am very proud of it and cannot imagine what it would be like to be an outsider living elsewhere.

My land is mostly a dry and dusty place. But through the middle runs the Great River, the most important river on Earth. During the winter and spring the River runs lower and lower. But in the summer the God of the Flood causes it to be reborn. It swells, bursting its banks to spread life-giving water over the fields on either side. From these fields come our wealth and our food.

The mighty Rameses, the greatest god-king of all, rules our land. Horus the Falcon God guides him and guards him, and beside him I am nothing but a speck of sand. Just like the River every year and the Sun every morning, after death His Majesty will be reborn. He will then be a god who lives for ever.

We also can be reborn into the Afterlife, the Field of Reeds. To do so we must worship the gods and keep our hearts pure. It's not easy, but I will try. Promise.

# Our journey

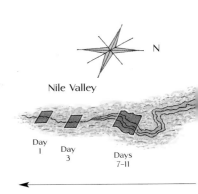

Hello. I'm Dedia, and this is a map of the brilliant adventure I had last year. As I had just turned 11, my dad, Captain Wennufer, said I should learn to help him at work. Delivering cargo as we went, we sailed down the Great River to the wedding of Uncle Nebre in Piramesse. Uncle is a scribe, very rich and important. Mum stayed behind to manage the household. One problem, though: Dad agreed to take my fierce Aunt Meritat and her know-all daughter Ipuia – not my favourite relations.

**Nile Valley**

Egyptian civilization flourished within the valley cut by the mighty River Nile as it snaked through the arid desert. In September, as the river's annual flood is subsiding, the river is still several metres deep and flowing as fast as a boy can run.

**DAY 10**

**Deir el-Medina**
The crowded village has been built to house workers from the Valley of the Kings.

**DAY 11**

**cemetery**
The last rites are being performed for the village's respected head man.

friend's house

Valley of the Queens

**DAY 1**

**Elephantine**
The journey starts here – the furthest south boats can sail without meeting rapids.

Wennufer's ship

Dedia's house

First cataract

desert

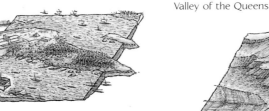

Thebes

edge of desert

**DAY 18**

**farmland**
Rich farmland is visible o both banks of the river.

tomb of Rameses II

quarry

**DAY 3**

**Gebel el-Silsila**
The stone from this quarry provides building material for use all over Egypt.

**DAY 7**

**Karnak**
Beside the broad waters of the Nile lies the most glorious temple in all Egypt.

Temple of Amun

**DAY 10**

**Valley of the Kings**
In this secret site of royal burials craftsmen are preparing a tomb for our king. His Majesty Rameses II.

## Nile Delta

Day 18
Day 22
Day 24
Day 30

800 km
500 miles

## The Egyptian calendar

The 360 normal days of the Egyptian year were divided into 12 equal months:

year   month   day

and into three seasons:

Inundation   winter   summer

Numbers were built up using symbols, an upside-down horseshoe representing 10. The calendar started afresh with each new reign. So 1278 BCE, the second year of the reign of Rameses II, was written like this:

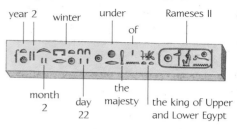

year 2   winter   under   Rameses II
                    of

month   day   the   the king of Upper
2       22    majesty   and Lower Egypt

Our story is set in the 48th year of the reign of Rameses II (1230 BCE).

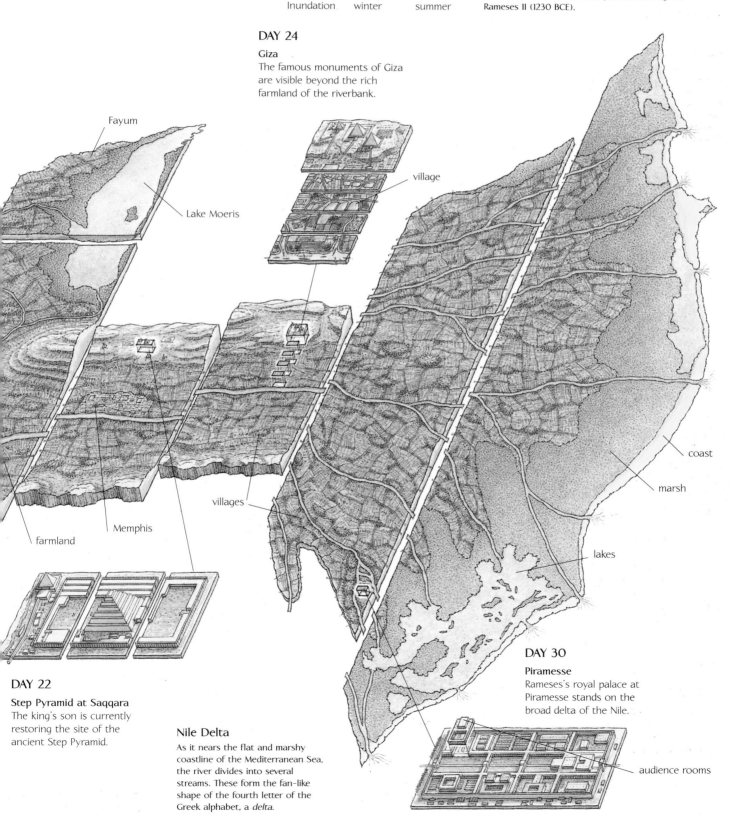

## DAY 24

### Giza
The famous monuments of Giza are visible beyond the rich farmland of the riverbank.

Fayum

Lake Moeris

village

villages

coast

marsh

Memphis

lakes

farmland

## DAY 22

### Step Pyramid at Saqqara
The king's son is currently restoring the site of the ancient Step Pyramid.

### Nile Delta
As it nears the flat and marshy coastline of the Mediterranean Sea, the river divides into several streams. These form the fan-like shape of the fourth letter of the Greek alphabet, a *delta*.

## DAY 30

### Piramesse
Rameses's royal palace at Piramesse stands on the broad delta of the Nile.

audience rooms

# The harbour at Elephantine

I'd often visited the docks at Elephantine, but only to watch. This time it was for real – I was actually setting off for Lower Egypt, the kingdom of the Red Crown. Feeling anxious, I clutched the amulet Mum had given me. I needed the gods' protection. One wish came true straightaway. Aunt Meritat and Cousin Ipuia were late. To keep to his tight schedule, Dad left without them. Hooray!

**amulet**
An amulet was a small magic charm worn to protect its owner from harm or to give them special powers.

**obelisk barge**
A gigantic barge, towed by smaller rowing boats, is transporting a 1000-tonne granite obelisk that has been cut from the nearby quarry.

mast

look-out

cabin of woven reeds

caged baboon

Dedia wearing amulet

steering oars

storehouses

trading ships

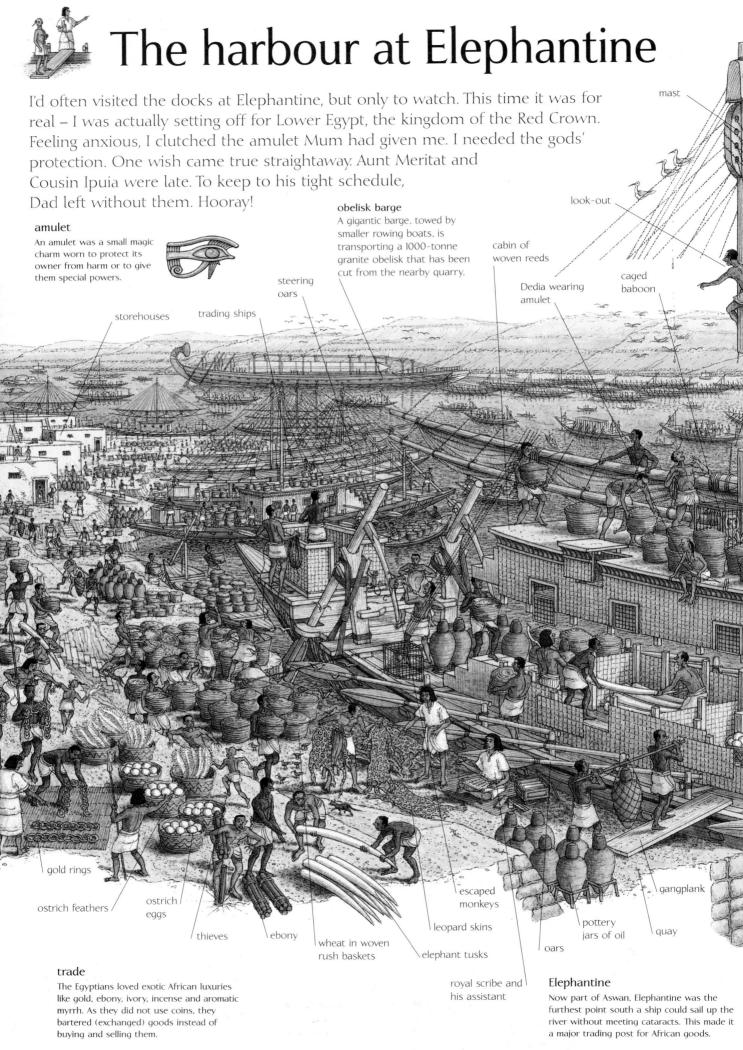

gold rings

ostrich feathers

ostrich eggs

thieves

ebony

wheat in woven rush baskets

elephant tusks

escaped monkeys

leopard skins

royal scribe and his assistant

oars

pottery jars of oil

gangplank

quay

**trade**
The Egyptians loved exotic African luxuries like gold, ebony, ivory, incense and aromatic myrrh. As they did not use coins, they bartered (exchanged) goods instead of buying and selling them.

**Elephantine**
Now part of Aswan, Elephantine was the furthest point south a ship could sail up the river without meeting cataracts. This made it a major trading post for African goods.

**cataracts**

The first of the Nile's six cataracts – rocky rapids impassable to ships – was just south of Elephantine. At a cataract a ship was hauled from the river and dragged to the next stretch of smooth water.

rope made from plant fibres

**Nilometer**

Nilometers accurately measure the height of the river. This one consists of steps which the water covers or reveals as it rises and falls. Nilometers may have been used to estimate taxes – a high flood might mean more arable land the next harvest, so increased taxes!

wealthy lady in her private barge

Day 1

**temple of Khnum**

The ram-headed potter god Khnum is Elephantine's main deity. Because rams are associated with fertility and potters with making things, Khnum is also seen as a creator god.

Khnum

rowers

palm trees

prisoners of war

ship's toilet

mud-sealed jars of incense

Wennufer

dom nuts

stone ballast to keep the ship upright

**ship construction**

Ships were made of long planks tied together over a skeleton of beams. Rectangular linen sails, mainly used for upstream travel, were hung between two wooden spars. Oars made the boat faster and helped with steering.

# Quarrying at Gebel el-Silsila

Our first stop was the Gebel el-Silsila stone quarries. While the stores were being unloaded, I wandered up to the quarry face. The skill of the workmen – many only slaves – was amazing. Imagine hacking out a block of stone exactly square – incredible! On my return, bad news: Aunt Meritat had taken another boat and caught us up. Worse still, Ipuia had brought along the most inconvenient wedding present. A live lion cub.

sailing upstream

baskets of grain – the workers' wages

Wennufer organizing the unloading of cargo

quay

**slavery**
Slaves were normally prisoners of war. They were not necessarily badly treated. Many worked as household servants, and fortunate ones even owned their own land.

**singing**
The oarsmen sing to help keep the rhythm of their rowing.

ferry

stone blocks being taken downstream

papyrus skiff

**fishing**
Fishing is an uncertain business. Some fish may not be caught because they are sacred – and the situation varies from region to region.

hippo

**hippo hunt**
Hippo hunting is a popular activity, although only males are supposed to be killed. The female hippo is associated with the household goddess Taweret, known as 'the great female'.

maid with ostrich-feather fan

lion cub

Aunt Meritat

Dedia

Ipuia

roast gazelle

ramp

linen awning

**crocodile attack**
Attack by Nile crocodiles is a real danger. Nevertheless, killing a crocodile is not approved of in areas that worship the crocodile god Sobek.

**tools**
In Dedia's time tools were made of stone, wood or bronze, a mixture of copper (about 90–95%) and tin (about 5–10%). A bronze chisel soon went blunt when it was hammered into stone.

sledge and levers

mason's mallet

wooden wedge

stone pounder

bronze or copper chisels

**quarry workers**
The back-breaking work of quarrying may be carried out by convicts or slaves. The more skilful tasks are done by trained workmen.

**dressing**
Mined blocks are dressed – cut to an exact shape. This involves hours of slow and painstaking work with a wooden mallet and bronze chisel.

metalworkers resharpening tools

Day 3

**mines and quarries**
Egypt had many mines and quarries. Some provided stone suitable for large buildings like pyramids or temples. Others provided minerals, such as natron and salt. The most valuable yielded metals and semi-precious stones.

**cutting a block**
1 rockface is measured into blocks
2 edges are marked with paint
3 narrow channels are hacked around the blocks
4 wooden wedges split the rock
5 rough blocks are hauled away to be dressed

accident!

hauling out a block

foreman organizes new batch of slaves

removing rubbish

lever

listening for stone to crack

hammering in wooden wedges

hacking out a block with stone pounders

painting lines

measuring a block

foreman

scribe

water pot

manoeuvring a block onto a sledge using wooden levers

**building materials**
Egypt's principal building materials were mud-brick, wood and stone. Gebel el-Silsila provided sandstone, which was easy to dig out. Limestone and basalt were other popular building stones. Granite, the toughest type of stone, was also the hardest to work.

**vital statistics**
A typical building block measuring 1000 mm x 1000 mm x 600 mm weighs about 2 tonnes.

# Amun-Ra's temple at Karnak

The temple at Karnak, our next stop, was awe-inspiring. It made me feel so small. We sensed the mighty Amun-Ra everywhere, as if he were watching us. Ipuia and I went with Dad to deliver the gold, ivory and leopard skins to the temple storeman. To lighten the atmosphere a bit, I asked the storeman if he'd like the skin of a lion cub, too. Sadly, he said no. Ipuia was livid!

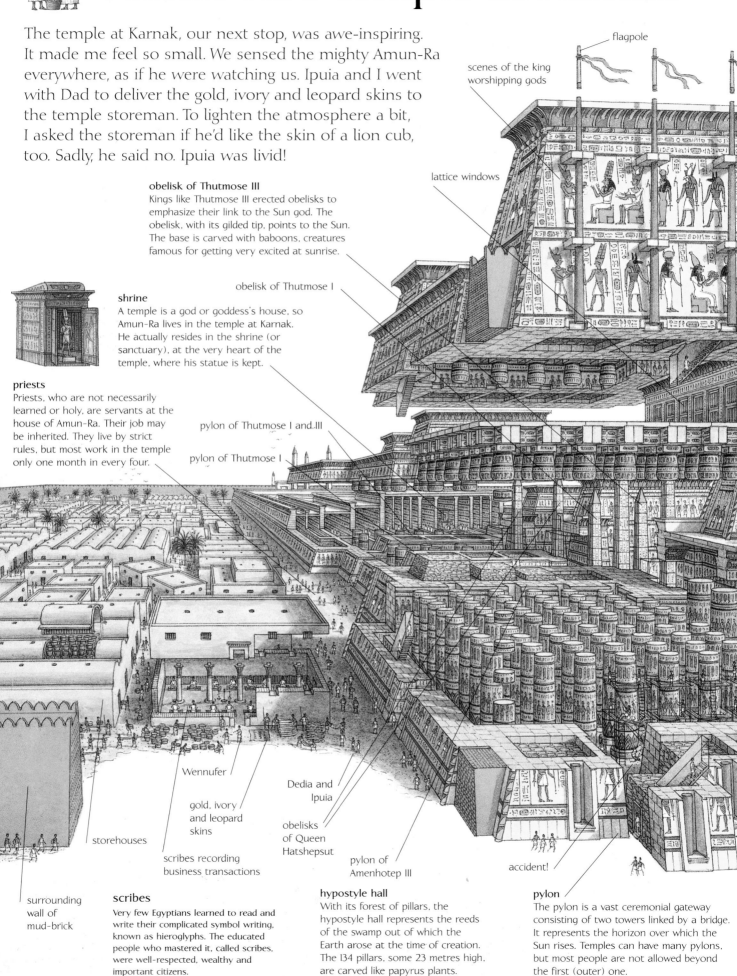

flagpole

scenes of the king worshipping gods

lattice windows

**obelisk of Thutmose III**
Kings like Thutmose III erected obelisks to emphasize their link to the Sun god. The obelisk, with its gilded tip, points to the Sun. The base is carved with baboons, creatures famous for getting very excited at sunrise.

obelisk of Thutmose I

**shrine**
A temple is a god or goddess's house, so Amun-Ra lives in the temple at Karnak. He actually resides in the shrine (or sanctuary), at the very heart of the temple, where his statue is kept.

**priests**
Priests, who are not necessarily learned or holy, are servants at the house of Amun-Ra. Their job may be inherited. They live by strict rules, but most work in the temple only one month in every four.

pylon of Thutmose I and III

pylon of Thutmose I

Wennufer

gold, ivory and leopard skins

storehouses

scribes recording business transactions

Dedia and Ipuia

obelisks of Queen Hatshepsut

pylon of Amenhotep III

accident!

surrounding wall of mud-brick

**scribes**
Very few Egyptians learned to read and write their complicated symbol writing, known as hieroglyphs. The educated people who mastered it, called scribes, were well-respected, wealthy and important citizens.

**hypostyle hall**
With its forest of pillars, the hypostyle hall represents the reeds of the swamp out of which the Earth arose at the time of creation. The 134 pillars, some 23 metres high, are carved like papyrus plants.

**pylon**
The pylon is a vast ceremonial gateway consisting of two towers linked by a bridge. It represents the horizon over which the Sun rises. Temples can have many pylons, but most people are not allowed beyond the first (outer) one.

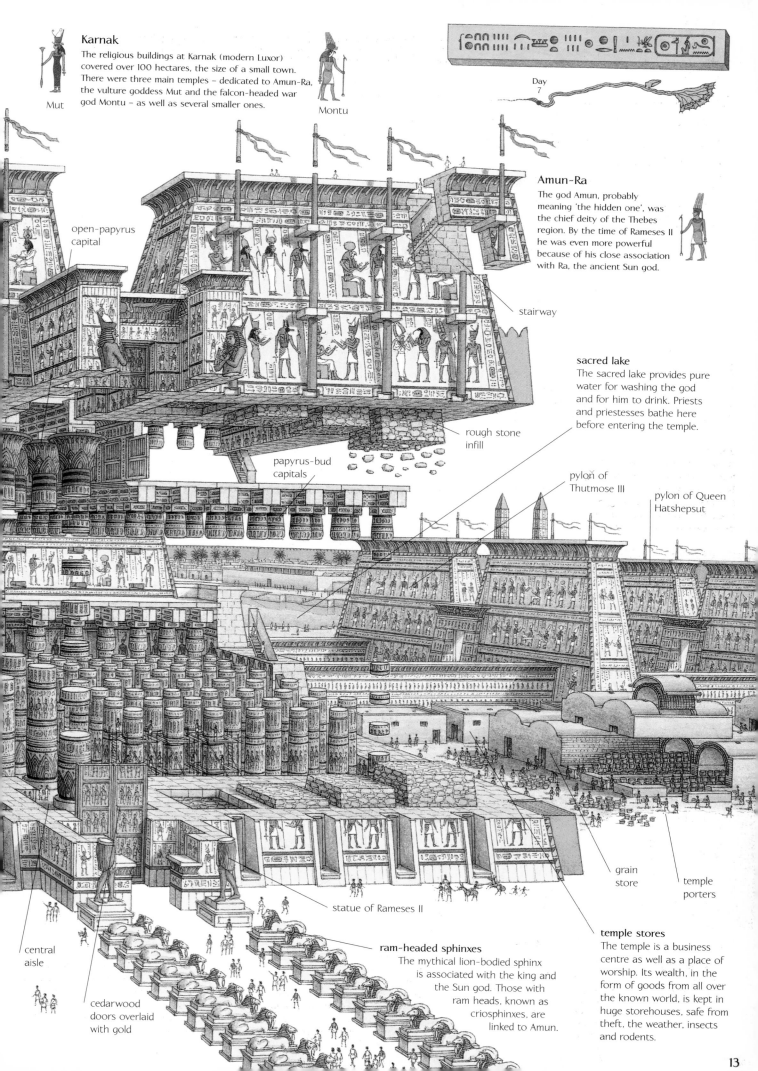

## Karnak

The religious buildings at Karnak (modern Luxor) covered over 100 hectares, the size of a small town. There were three main temples – dedicated to Amun-Ra, the vulture goddess Mut and the falcon-headed war god Montu – as well as several smaller ones.

Mut

Montu

Day 7

## Amun-Ra

The god Amun, probably meaning 'the hidden one', was the chief deity of the Thebes region. By the time of Rameses II he was even more powerful because of his close association with Ra, the ancient Sun god.

open-papyrus capital

stairway

sacred lake
The sacred lake provides pure water for washing the god and for him to drink. Priests and priestesses bathe here before entering the temple.

rough stone infill

papyrus-bud capitals

pylon of Thutmose III

pylon of Queen Hatshepsut

statue of Rameses II

grain store

temple porters

central aisle

cedarwood doors overlaid with gold

ram-headed sphinxes
The mythical lion-bodied sphinx is associated with the king and the Sun god. Those with ram heads, known as criosphinxes, are linked to Amun.

temple stores
The temple is a business centre as well as a place of worship. Its wealth, in the form of goods from all over the known world, is kept in huge storehouses, safe from theft, the weather, insects and rodents.

13

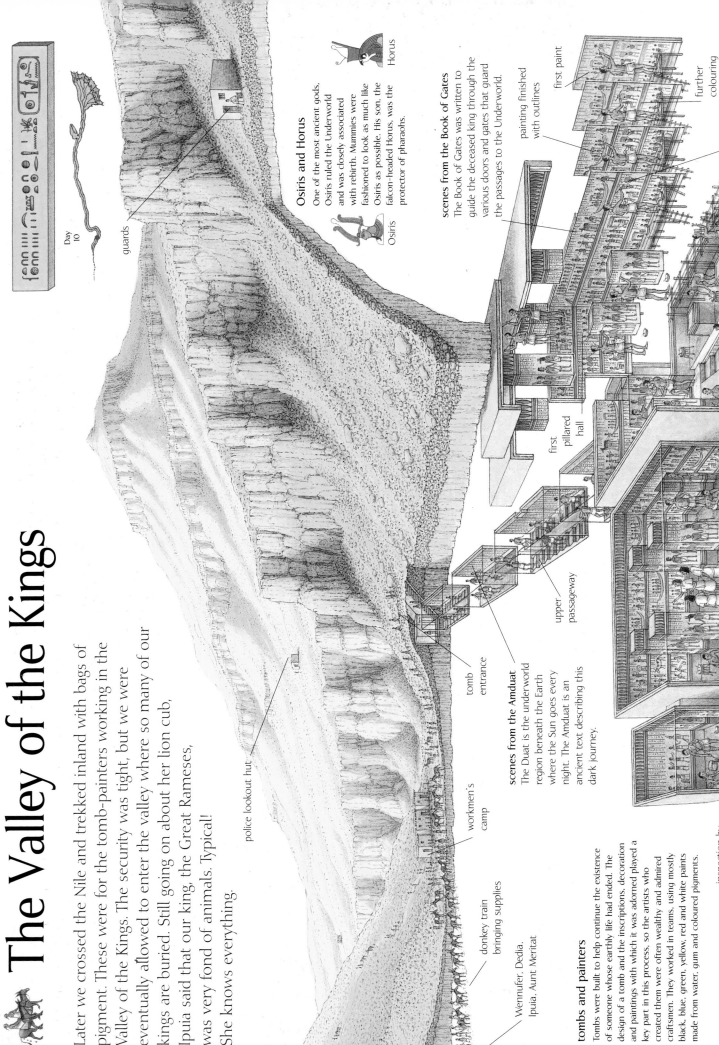

# The Valley of the Kings

Later we crossed the Nile and trekked inland with bags of pigment. These were for the tomb-painters working in the Valley of the Kings. The security was tight, but we were eventually allowed to enter the valley where so many of our kings are buried. Still going on about her lion cub, Ipuia said that our king, the Great Rameses, was very fond of animals. Typical! She knows everything.

Day 10

guards

## Osiris and Horus

Horus

Osiris

One of the most ancient gods, Osiris ruled the Underworld and was closely associated with rebirth. Mummies were fashioned to look as much like Osiris as possible. His son, the falcon-headed Horus, was the protector of pharaohs.

## scenes from the Book of Gates

The Book of Gates was written to guide the deceased king through the various doors and gates that guard the passages to the Underworld.

first paint

painting finished with outlines

further colouring

first pillared hall

upper passageway

tomb entrance

## scenes from the Amduat

The Duat is the underworld region beneath the Earth where the Sun goes every night. The Amduat is an ancient text describing this dark journey.

police lookout hut

workmen's camp

donkey train bringing supplies

Wennufer. Dedia. Ipuia. Aunt Meritat.

## tombs and painters

Tombs were built to help continue the existence of someone whose earthly life had ended. The design of a tomb and the inscriptions, decoration and paintings with which it was adorned played a key part in this process, so the artists who created them were often wealthy and admired craftsmen. They worked in teams, using mostly black, blue, green, yellow, red and white paints made from water, gum and coloured pigments.

inspection by

14

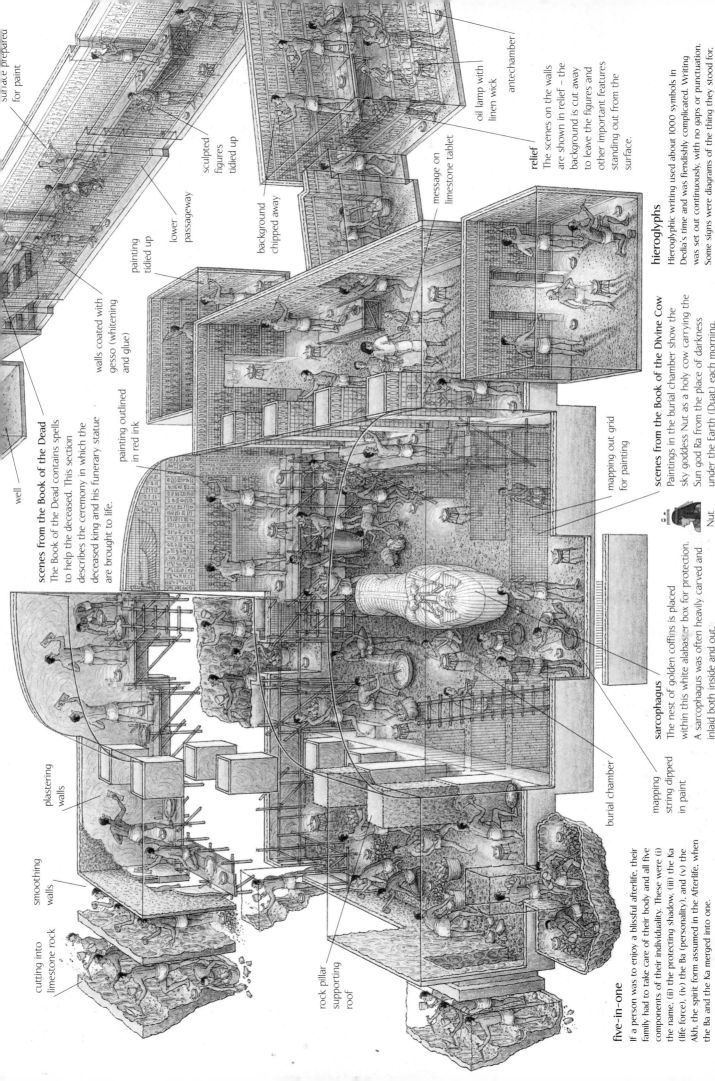

surface prepared for paint

well

scenes from the Book of the Dead
The Book of the Dead contains spells to help the deceased. This section describes the ceremony in which the deceased king and his funerary statue are brought to life.

walls coated with gesso (whitening and glue)

painting outlined in red ink

painting tidied up

sculpted figures tidied up

lower passageway

background chipped away

message on limestone tablet

oil lamp with linen wick

antechamber

relief
The scenes on the walls are shown in relief – the background is cut away to leave the figures and other important features standing out from the surface.

hieroglyphs
Hieroglyphic writing used about 1000 symbols in Dedia's time and was fiendishly complicated. Writing was set out continuously, with no gaps or punctuation. Some signs were diagrams of the thing they stood for, others represented sounds or ideas.

mapping out grid for painting

scenes from the Book of the Divine Cow
Paintings in the burial chamber show the sky goddess Nut as a holy cow carrying the Sun god Ra from the place of darkness under the Earth (Duat) each morning.

Nut

plastering walls

smoothing walls

cutting into limestone rock

five-in-one
If a person was to enjoy a blissful afterlife, their family had to take care of their body and all five components of their individuality. These were (i) the name, (ii) the protecting shadow, (iii) the Ka (life force), (iv) the Ba (personality), and (v) the Akh, the spirit form assumed in the Afterlife, when the Ba and the Ka merged into one.

rock pillar supporting roof

mapping string dipped in paint

burial chamber

sarcophagus
The nest of golden coffins is placed within this white alabaster box for protection. A sarcophagus was often heavily carved and inlaid both inside and out.

# Deir el-Medina stop-over

After the Valley of the Kings, Aunt Meritat was tired and Ipuia missed her lion cub. They returned to the boat with their servants, while Dad and I visited Deir el-Medina. We called on an old merchant friend of Dad's. He made us really welcome and insisted we stay the night. It was quite a relief to get away from Ipuia's running commentary on everyone and everything we saw.

**toys**
Egyptian children played with simple toys such as balls, dolls, spinning tops and model animals.

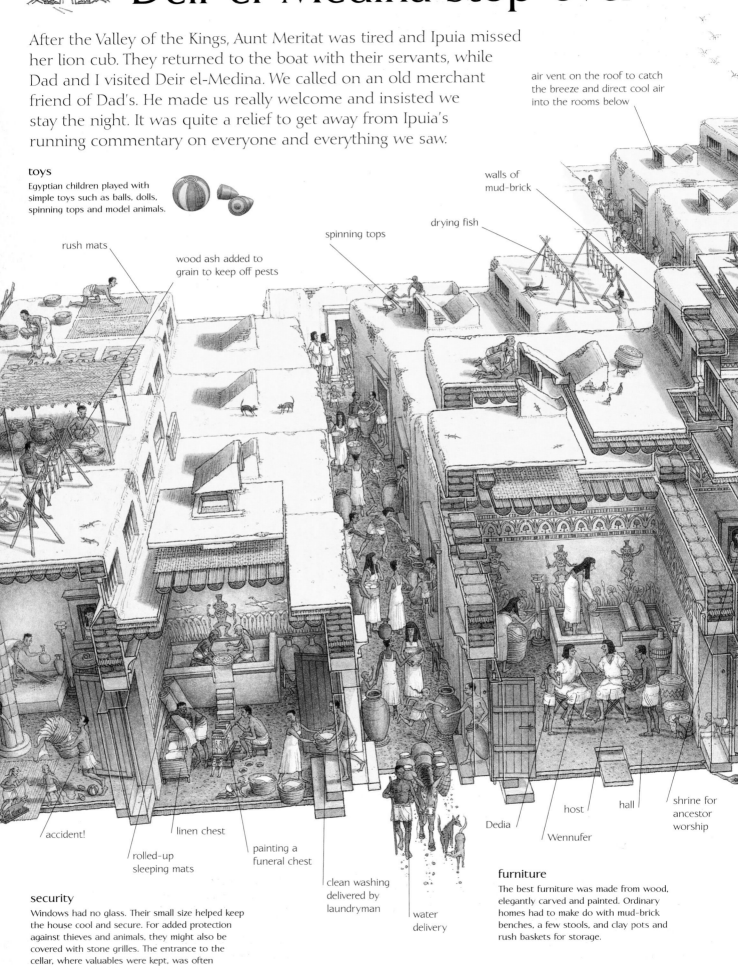

air vent on the roof to catch the breeze and direct cool air into the rooms below

walls of mud-brick

drying fish

spinning tops

rush mats

wood ash added to grain to keep off pests

accident!

linen chest

rolled-up sleeping mats

painting a funeral chest

clean washing delivered by laundryman

water delivery

Dedia

Wennufer

host

hall

shrine for ancestor worship

**security**
Windows had no glass. Their small size helped keep the house cool and secure. For added protection against thieves and animals, they might also be covered with stone grilles. The entrance to the cellar, where valuables were kept, was often protected by placing a bed over it.

**furniture**
The best furniture was made from wood, elegantly carved and painted. Ordinary homes had to make do with mud-brick benches, a few stools, and clay pots and rush baskets for storage.

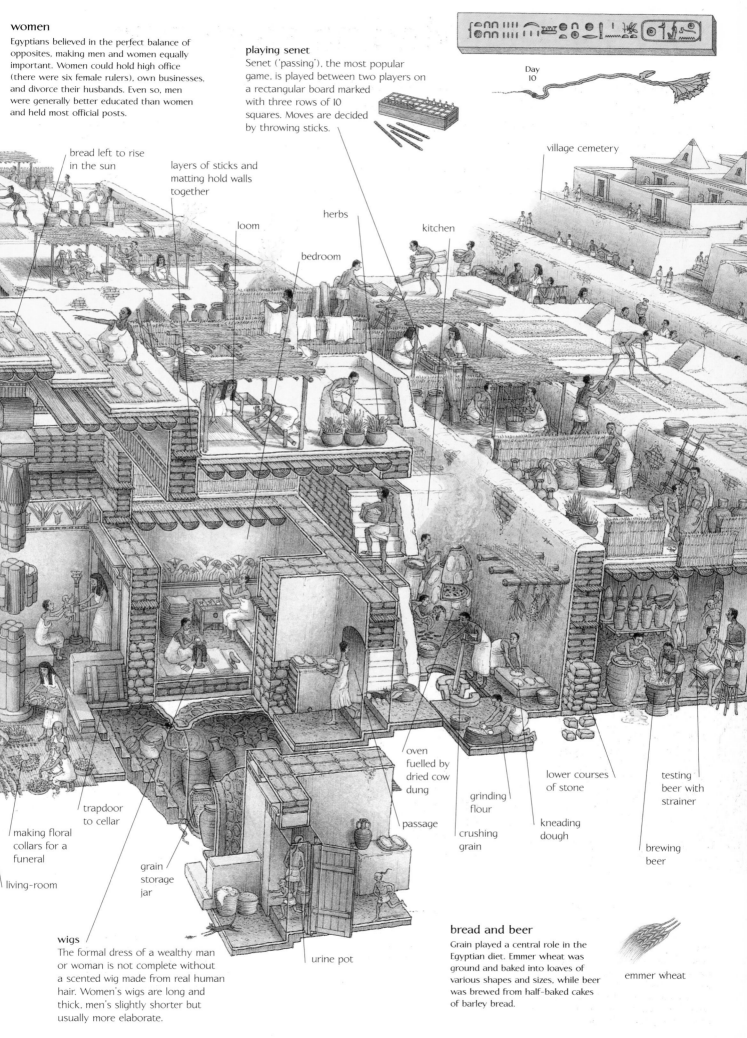

## women

Egyptians believed in the perfect balance of opposites, making men and women equally important. Women could hold high office (there were six female rulers), own businesses, and divorce their husbands. Even so, men were generally better educated than women and held most official posts.

## playing senet

Senet ('passing'), the most popular game, is played between two players on a rectangular board marked with three rows of 10 squares. Moves are decided by throwing sticks.

Day
10

bread left to rise in the sun

layers of sticks and matting hold walls together

loom

herbs

bedroom

kitchen

village cemetery

making floral collars for a funeral

living-room

trapdoor to cellar

grain storage jar

oven fuelled by dried cow dung

passage

grinding flour

crushing grain

kneading dough

lower courses of stone

testing beer with strainer

brewing beer

urine pot

## wigs

The formal dress of a wealthy man or woman is not complete without a scented wig made from real human hair. Women's wigs are long and thick, men's slightly shorter but usually more elaborate.

## bread and beer

Grain played a central role in the Egyptian diet. Emmer wheat was ground and baked into loaves of various shapes and sizes, while beer was brewed from half-baked cakes of barley bread.

emmer wheat

17

# A funeral at Deir el-Medina

The next day Deir el-Medina held the funeral of its head man. As a mark of respect, Dad and I stayed to take part. The official's corpse had been prepared during the weeks since he had died. The priests organized the ceremony with meticulous detail. Everything that made him what he was – his body, soul, spirit, name and shadow – were cared for. He was sure to enjoy his next life.

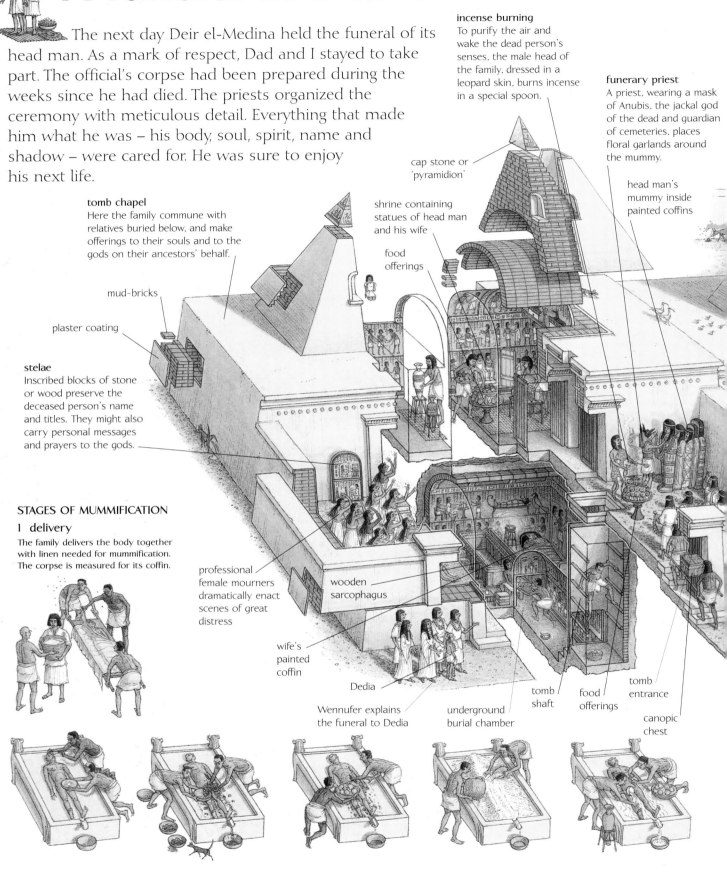

**incense burning**
To purify the air and wake the dead person's senses, the male head of the family, dressed in a leopard skin, burns incense in a special spoon.

**funerary priest**
A priest, wearing a mask of Anubis, the jackal god of the dead and guardian of cemeteries, places floral garlands around the mummy.

**cap stone or 'pyramidion'**

**shrine containing statues of head man and his wife**

**food offerings**

**head man's mummy inside painted coffins**

**tomb chapel**
Here the family commune with relatives buried below, and make offerings to their souls and to the gods on their ancestors' behalf.

**mud-bricks**

**plaster coating**

**stelae**
Inscribed blocks of stone or wood preserve the deceased person's name and titles. They might also carry personal messages and prayers to the gods.

**professional female mourners** dramatically enact scenes of great distress

**wooden sarcophagus**

**wife's painted coffin**

**Dedia**

**Wennufer explains the funeral to Dedia**

**underground burial chamber**

**tomb shaft**

**food offerings**

**tomb entrance**

**canopic chest**

## STAGES OF MUMMIFICATION

### 1 delivery
The family delivers the body together with linen needed for mummification. The corpse is measured for its coffin.

### 2 de-braining
After the body has been laid out on a stone table, the brain is often removed through the nose with hooks. The inside of the skull is then washed out.

### 3 gutting
The corpse is cut open down the left side and the internal organs (except the heart and kidneys) are removed for separate preservation.

### 4 washing and stuffing
The body is washed with fragrant palm wine before the inner cavity is stuffed with water-absorbing natron and a temporary packing.

### 5 drying
To remove all vestiges of rot-inducing moisture, the body is covered with natron and left for 40 days.

### 6 cleaning and packing
Using Nile water, traces of natron are cleaned from the dried-out (desiccated) corpse. The empty body cavity is packed with sawdust and linen rags, and the head with resin-soaked linen.

## journey to the Afterlife

In a final judgement after death, a person's heart was balanced against the feather of Maat (truth) to see if they were worthy of entering the Afterlife. The hearts of those who failed were flung to a hideous monster known as the 'Devourer'. Those who succeeded were allowed to proceed to the Field of Reeds, the kingdom of Osiris.

**grave goods**
A dead person was provided with just about everything they might need in the next world, from clothes to jewellery.

**villagers make their way to the funeral feast**

**clay seals**
Often stamped with the image of Anubis, seals protect the locked doors to the tomb.

**canopic chest**
The corpse's internal organs (except the heart and kidneys, which are left in the body) have been mummified and stored in canopic jars. These are assembled in the canopic chest.

**courtyard**

**white ox and sledge return to the village after delivering the coffin**

**friends and relatives, wearing white head bands, prepare to escort the body**

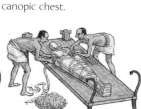

### 7 oiling
The body is transferred to a wooden table. Here its skin is rubbed with oils, the nose holes plugged, the eye sockets padded out, and a final coating of resin applied.

### 8 wrapping
Reciting spells at each stage, the embalmers start to bandage the body, beginning with the limbs.

### 9 protecting
In a process that takes many days, the entire corpse is wrapped in hundreds of metres of linen bandages. Protective amulets are placed within the bandaging.

### 10 securing
The well-wrapped corpse is secured with linen cords and placed within a linen shroud.

### 11 finishing
Adorned with a painted face mask, the body is lowered into its coffin. The jackal-headed priest places a papyrus Book of the Dead beside the body.

# Saqqara's Step Pyramid

After Karnak, we sailed to Memphis to pick up a very important passenger: the regional governor. He was going to Piramesse to meet the king. As he wasn't ready when we arrived, we went on a sight-seeing trip to Saqqara, to visit the pyramid tombs of the ancient kings of Egypt. The massive repair works of Prince Khaemwaset made the place look a bit of a tip. Needless to say, Ipuia knew all about everything – except the ancient graffiti, which I found.

### Step Pyramid
The first pyramid was built King Djoser. Starting as a s mastaba, six massive 'steps were added to create a pyramid 60 metres high.

### pyramid restoration
By the time of Rameses II, the Saqqara pyramid complex was over 1000 years old. The king's fourth son, Khaemwaset, made a name for himself by restoring this and other monuments. It was a way of showing respect for his royal predecessors.

### burial chamber
The mummified body, its coffin and sarcophagus are laid deep in the burial chamber to keep them safe from robbers. The interior of King Unas's pyramid also contains the earliest-known pyramid texts – spells to help the deceased in various ways. Some of the texts were echoed in the later Book of the Dead.

### pyramid construction
People have long wondered how pyramids were raised to such a height. The answer is probably that a massive ramp of earth, built alongside the pyramid site, was used to drag the building blocks into place.

### mortuary temple
Deceased kings were gods. While alive, they built mortuary temples in which they could be worshipped after their death, and in which offerings could be made to sustain them in the next life.

pyramid of King Unas

passage to burial chamber

### injured worker
A construction-site doctor treats a worker with a broken arm. Egyptian doctors were skilled at dealing with fractures and similar injuries.

dead labourer

foreman

boat

### boat pit of King Unas
As gods travel in holy barges, boats were buried near the king (who has become a god) for his use in the Afterlife.

supplies

causeway of Unas

relief carving

carpenters

workmen's camp and storage area

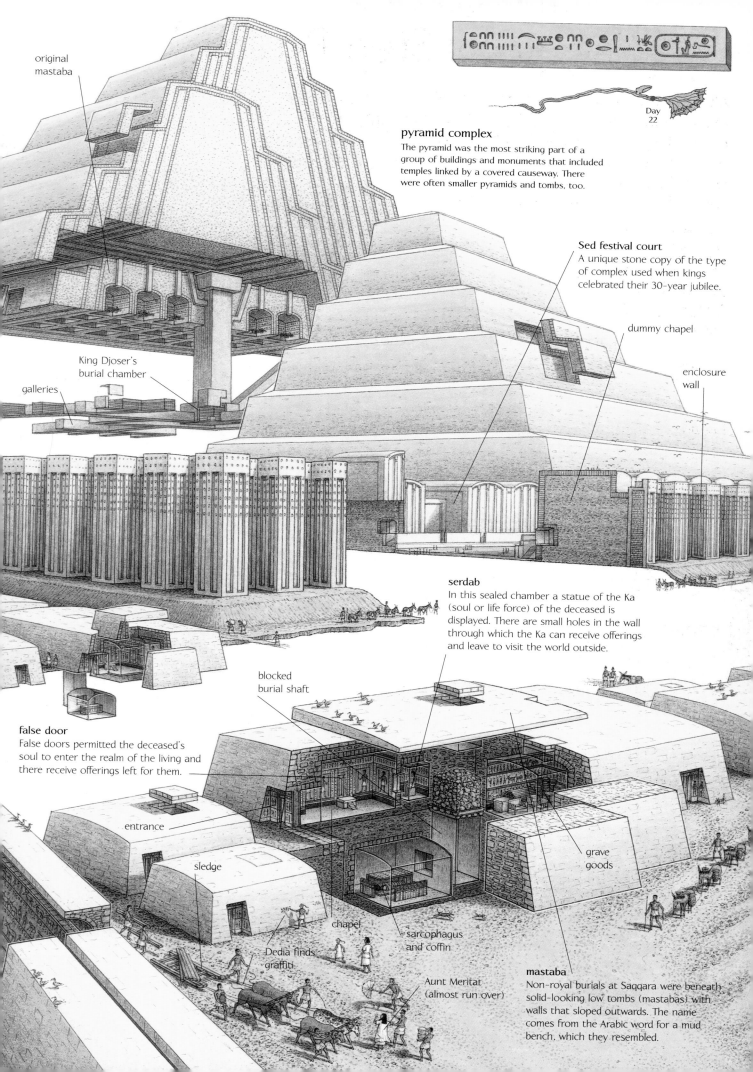

original mastaba

## pyramid complex
The pyramid was the most striking part of a group of buildings and monuments that included temples linked by a covered causeway. There were often smaller pyramids and tombs, too.

### Sed festival court
A unique stone copy of the type of complex used when kings celebrated their 30-year jubilee.

dummy chapel

enclosure wall

King Djoser's burial chamber

galleries

### serdab
In this sealed chamber a statue of the Ka (soul or life force) of the deceased is displayed. There are small holes in the wall through which the Ka can receive offerings and leave to visit the world outside.

blocked burial shaft

### false door
False doors permitted the deceased's soul to enter the realm of the living and there receive offerings left for them.

grave goods

entrance

sledge

chapel

sarcophagus and coffin

Dedia finds graffiti

Aunt Meritat (almost run over)

### mastaba
Non-royal burials at Saqqara were beneath solid-looking low tombs (mastabas) with walls that sloped outwards. The name comes from the Arabic word for a mud bench, which they resembled.

# The fertile Nile

As we sailed on, I watched farmers recovering their fields and preparing them for sowing. One morning, as we were passing the pyramids and sphinx of Giza, the governor spoke to me. His Majesty, he said, was fond of animals. Would we like to offer him the lion cub? Without thinking, I said I'd be delighted. When I pointed out that it was Ipuia's, the governor smiled and said he'd settle things.

**The Sphinx of Giza**
'Sphinx' may have meant 'living image', and the largest and best-known example probably shows the face of King Khafra. 73 metres long and 20 metres high, it was originally carved from a single rocky outcrop. Workers are seen here replacing the Sphinx's beard.

**marking out the fields**
As the Inundation has washed away all the old field boundaries, they are measured out again by officials known as 'rope stretchers'.

villa

**brick-making**
Bricks are made with Nile mud reinforced with straw or chaff left over from threshing. They are not kiln-baked but simply left to dry out in the hot sun.

dried bricks

**sowing**
Wheat and barley are sown by scattering the seeds on the ground. They are then trampled in by goats.

**trapping birds**
Birds like wild duck and geese are a good source of meat. Hunting them is a popular sport, too.

**ploughing**
Because the flood soil is muddy and loose, teams of people or cows easily pull light wooden ploughs.

**throwing stick**
Birds are caught in nets or hunted with special wooden sticks that can be accurately thrown with great force.

fishing

rubble for repair work

lion cub

Wennufer

Aunt Meritat

governor

Dedia

Ipuia

**the Inundation**
Egypt was totally dependent on the annual flood (inundation) of the River Nile. This followed heavy rains in central Africa, far to the south, and left deposits of rich soil on either bank. Around Memphis the flood was highest in early September.

**plumbing**
A sailor checks the depth with a weight on the end of a plumb line. If a ship went aground when the river was falling, it might be stuck a long time!

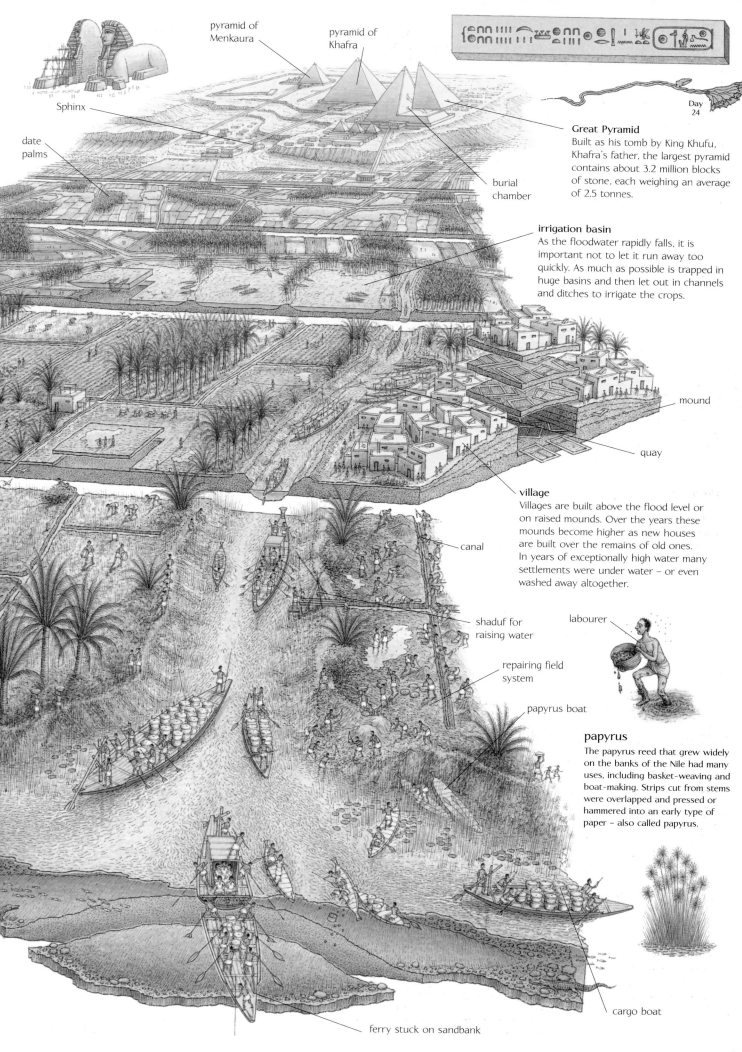

pyramid of
Menkaura

pyramid of
Khafra

Sphinx

date
palms

burial
chamber

### Great Pyramid
Built as his tomb by King Khufu,
Khafra's father, the largest pyramid
contains about 3.2 million blocks
of stone, each weighing an average
of 2.5 tonnes.

### irrigation basin
As the floodwater rapidly falls, it is
important not to let it run away too
quickly. As much as possible is trapped in
huge basins and then let out in channels
and ditches to irrigate the crops.

mound

quay

### village
Villages are built above the flood level or
on raised mounds. Over the years these
mounds become higher as new houses
are built over the remains of old ones.
In years of exceptionally high water many
settlements were under water – or even
washed away altogether.

canal

shaduf for
raising water

labourer

repairing field
system

papyrus boat

### papyrus
The papyrus reed that grew widely
on the banks of the Nile had many
uses, including basket-weaving and
boat-making. Strips cut from stems
were overlapped and pressed or
hammered into an early type of
paper – also called papyrus.

cargo boat

ferry stuck on sandbank

# Rameses's palace at Piramesse

How did the governor settle things with Ipuia? At Piramesse he arranged for us to present the lion cub to His Majesty *in person!* Walking through the palace courtyards, lying before the throne, hearing that voice – it was unforgettable. What's more, His Majesty presented Ipuia with a brilliant necklace. Afterwards, having shared so many adventures together, Ipuia and I actually became quite good friends. And we still are.

### Rameses the Great
Rameses II is known as 'the Great' because, during his extraordinary 67-year reign, he constructed or took over a vast number and range of buildings (mostly in honour of Rameses II himself) all over Egypt.

### throne room
The throne room is like the inner sanctuary of a temple, with the king-god himself seated on a raised platform at the far end.

### pharaoh
The importance of the king's palace (*per-aa* or 'great house') is shown by the fact that the name eventually became the title of the king himself – pharaoh.

### daughter–wife
Bint Anath, the king's favourite wife (also his daughter), sits on his left.

fan-bearer

### floor tiles
The floor tiles are decorated with images of the king's enemies so that everyone entering walks all over them!

### instruments
The Egyptians loved music and played a variety of instruments: percussion (e.g. drums and tambourines), wind (e.g. flutes), and stringed (e.g. lutes).

### pillared hall
The entire palace, but especially the pillared hall, is decorated with scenes that remind the viewer that the king is the source of fertility, wealth and plenty.

rush matting

mud-plaster coating

governor and lion cub

Wennufer

Dedia and Ipuia

dancers

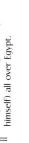

Day 30

24

**tribute**
Foreigners deliver tribute. Like other powerful kings, Rameses demands regular payment from the subject peoples within his widespread empire.

**courtiers**
The royal court was like a small village. It was populated by the royal family, high priests, nobles, scribes, officials, entertainers, guards and servants.

**palace pool**
Complete with ducks, fish and water lilies, the pool is an echo of the sacredness of water in a barren land.

date palm

mandrake

ivory

inlaid pavement

palm-style columns around courtyard

**palace guard**
Rameses can call on an enormous army of perhaps 20,000 soldiers. Only the élite, however, are selected to join his personal bodyguard.

standard bearer

bugler

drummer

gold

pomegranate tree

ostrich

**entertainment**
Because their religion paid so much attention to death and rebirth, Egyptian civilization might be thought rather gloomy. Far from it! The royal court was alive with every type of delight, from dancing to board games, juggling and book collecting.

**royal menagerie**
Rameses was famous for his collection of wild animals (menagerie) – which really did include a lion cub!

baboons

# ROME

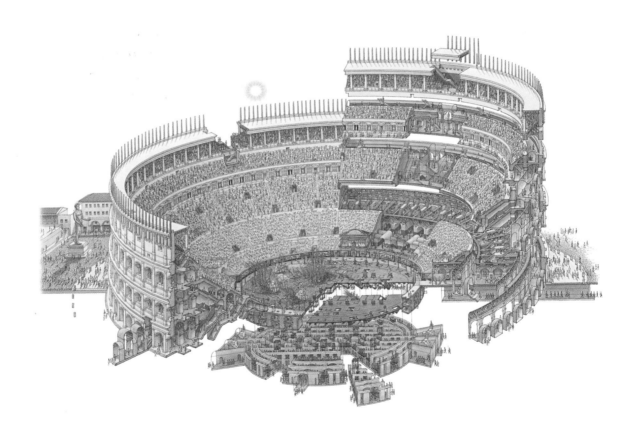

# Titus Cotta and Marcus Cotta Maximus

Titus Cotta is the son of an important Roman senator called Marcus Cotta Maximus. They live in a smart house on the Viminal Hill, not far from the centre of Rome. Titus doesn't go to school; he has lessons with his own tutor. But today is a festival day so there are no lessons. Titus and his father have a busy day planned…

# Rome, AD 128

This is the city of Rome in the year AD 128. It's the biggest city in the ancient world – over a million people live here. And it's at the centre of a huge empire stretching all the way from Egypt to Britain.

Today is the festival of the twin gods Castor and Pollux. There's a procession this morning, so people are making an early start. One of them is Titus Cotta Maximus. His father, Marcus, has promised to take him to the Colosseum and to the chariot races…

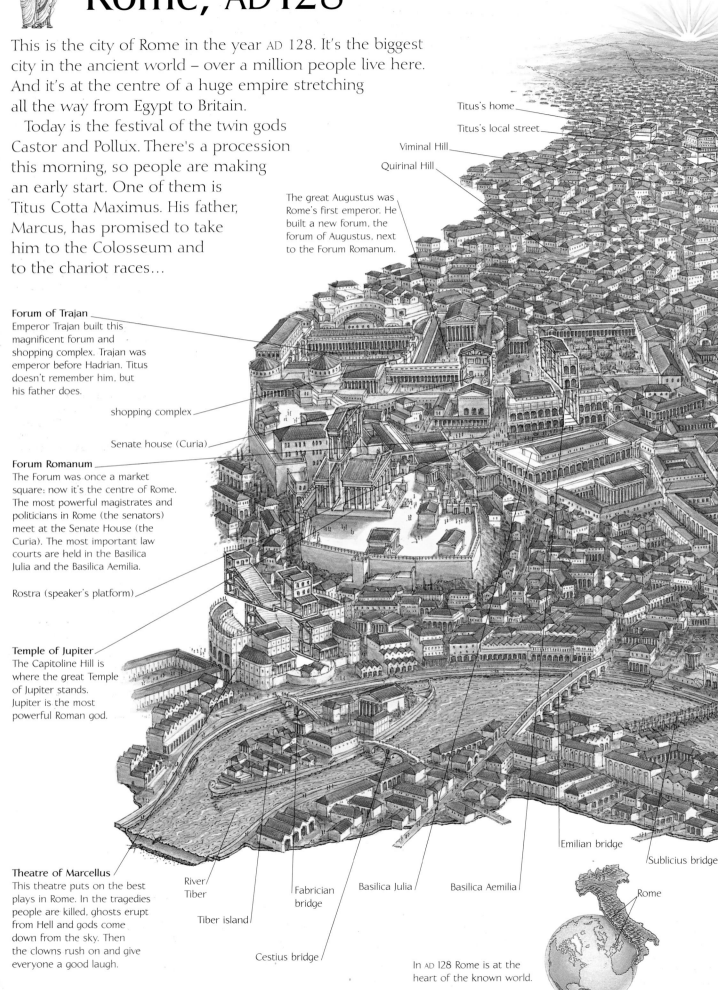

Titus's home

Titus's local street

Viminal Hill

Quirinal Hill

The great Augustus was Rome's first emperor. He built a new forum, the forum of Augustus, next to the Forum Romanum.

**Forum of Trajan**
Emperor Trajan built this magnificent forum and shopping complex. Trajan was emperor before Hadrian. Titus doesn't remember him, but his father does.

shopping complex

Senate house (Curia)

**Forum Romanum**
The Forum was once a market square: now it's the centre of Rome. The most powerful magistrates and politicians in Rome (the senators) meet at the Senate House (the Curia). The most important law courts are held in the Basilica Julia and the Basilica Aemilia.

Rostra (speaker's platform)

**Temple of Jupiter**
The Capitoline Hill is where the great Temple of Jupiter stands. Jupiter is the most powerful Roman god.

**Theatre of Marcellus**
This theatre puts on the best plays in Rome. In the tragedies people are killed, ghosts erupt from Hell and gods come down from the sky. Then the clowns rush on and give everyone a good laugh.

River Tiber

Fabrician bridge

Tiber island

Basilica Julia

Basilica Aemilia

Emilian bridge

Sublicius bridge

Rome

Cestius bridge

In AD 128 Rome is at the heart of the known world.

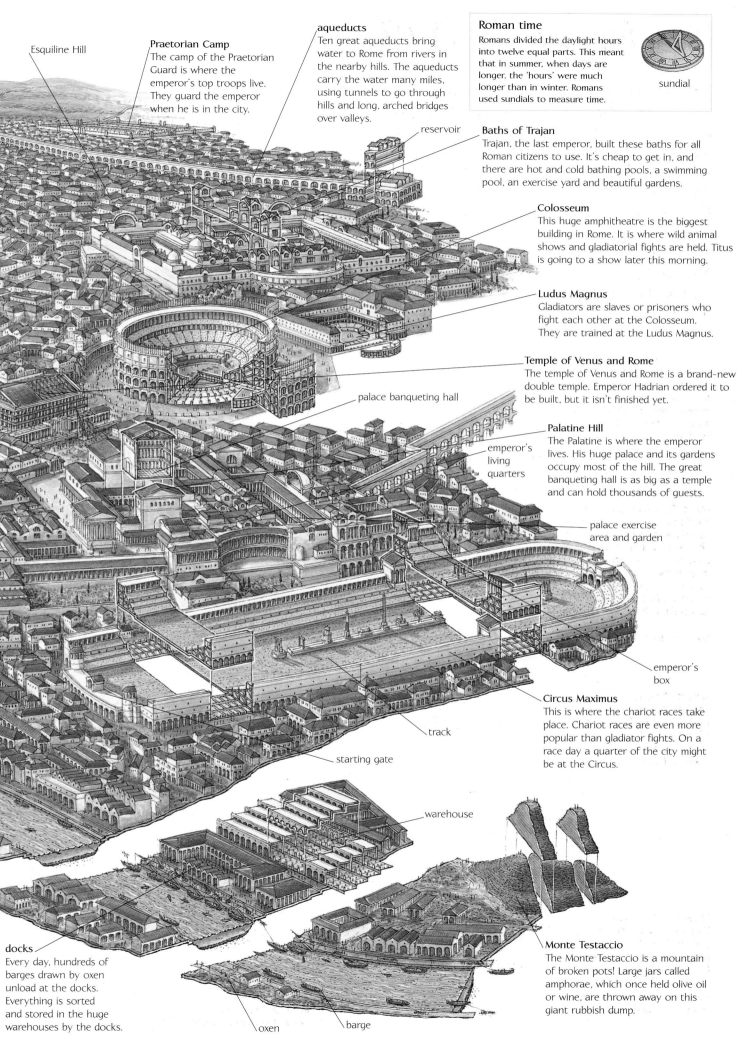

Esquiline Hill

**Praetorian Camp**
The camp of the Praetorian Guard is where the emperor's top troops live. They guard the emperor when he is in the city.

**aqueducts**
Ten great aqueducts bring water to Rome from rivers in the nearby hills. The aqueducts carry the water many miles, using tunnels to go through hills and long, arched bridges over valleys.

reservoir

**Baths of Trajan**
Trajan, the last emperor, built these baths for all Roman citizens to use. It's cheap to get in, and there are hot and cold bathing pools, a swimming pool, an exercise yard and beautiful gardens.

**Colosseum**
This huge amphitheatre is the biggest building in Rome. It is where wild animal shows and gladiatorial fights are held. Titus is going to a show later this morning.

**Ludus Magnus**
Gladiators are slaves or prisoners who fight each other at the Colosseum. They are trained at the Ludus Magnus.

**Temple of Venus and Rome**
The temple of Venus and Rome is a brand-new double temple. Emperor Hadrian ordered it to be built, but it isn't finished yet.

palace banqueting hall

emperor's living quarters

**Palatine Hill**
The Palatine is where the emperor lives. His huge palace and its gardens occupy most of the hill. The great banqueting hall is as big as a temple and can hold thousands of guests.

palace exercise area and garden

emperor's box

**Circus Maximus**
This is where the chariot races take place. Chariot races are even more popular than gladiator fights. On a race day a quarter of the city might be at the Circus.

track

starting gate

warehouse

**docks**
Every day, hundreds of barges drawn by oxen unload at the docks. Everything is sorted and stored in the huge warehouses by the docks.

oxen

barge

**Monte Testaccio**
The Monte Testaccio is a mountain of broken pots! Large jars called amphorae, which once held olive oil or wine, are thrown away on this giant rubbish dump.

# Titus's house

It's only just light, but at Titus's house everyone is busy. As today is a festival day, Titus and his father will be out for the whole day, going to the Temple of Jupiter and visiting the games and the races. Titus's mother and baby sister stay at home. In the evening the family is going to host a festival day feast to celebrate.

**atrium**
The first room you come into is the atrium. This is a large hallway, with a small pool in the centre. Around the atrium there are stone carvings of Titus's ancestors.

carvings (busts) of ancestors

**doorway**
At night, the front door is guarded by a household slave with a guard dog. Titus's family are rich, so they have many slaves. Slaves can be bought and sold at slave markets. They do most of the work about the house.

clients

**water supply**
Titus's family is lucky – they have a well in the house. Not many Roman houses have their own water supply.

bronzesmith's shop

rainwater spouts

**shops**
The two rooms that face the street are rented out as shops. The owners sleep above the shop at night. This morning they are already hard at work.

street

pool (*impluvium*)

mosaic floor

slave

pet cat

**Titus**
Titus isn't dressed yet. The cook gave Titus some bread for breakfast. He gives a piece to his cat.

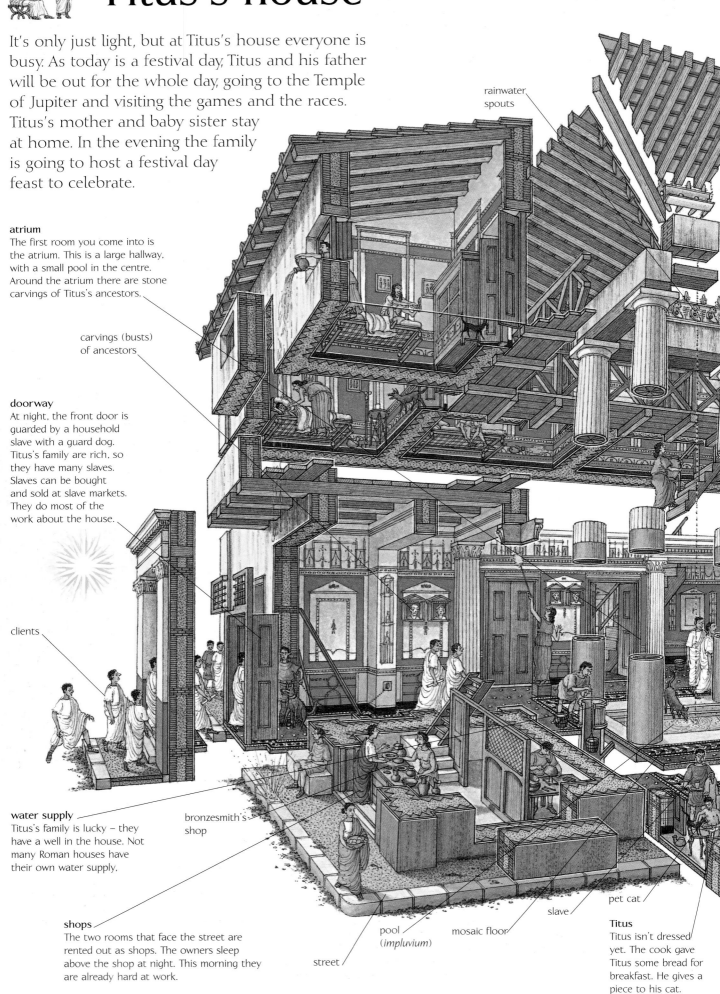

**atrium roof**
The roof of the atrium is wood, covered with clay tiles. When it rains, water drains through a hole in the roof into the pool in the atrium.

tiles

wooden roof beams

Livia's bedroom

**Family and household**
Many people live in Titus's house. As well as Titus's immediate family, there are his grandmother Cornelia and his aunt Maria (they are away at the moment at the family's country villa). There are also twenty slaves and servants! Chilo, the cook, is the most valuable slave in the house. His cooking is famous throughout Rome.

Marcus

Livia        Cornelia        Maria

Titus    Fulvia

Decimus
(Marcus's
secretary)

Nicander
(Titus's tutor)

Chilo
(the cook)

Potita
(Fulvia's
nurse)

Martilla (Livia's ornatrix,
or hairdresser)

Other household slaves

During the
1st hour
(6.30 a.m.)

**toilet**
The toilet is next to the kitchen. Waste water from the sink is used to flush it.

sponge stick
(this served
instead of
toilet paper)

sponge pot

toilet

water fountain

drain

slaves' rooms

kitchen

oven

fireplace

shrine of the household gods (*lararium*)

C IVL
POLYB
AED C

**baby Fulvia**
Fulvia is Titus's new baby sister. Titus has two grown-up sisters, too, but they are married and don't live at home.

bedroom

**Marcus**
Marcus, Titus's father, is seeing clients in the office. The clients are people who are less well-off than him. He helps them out, and sometimes finds them jobs. In return, they help him when there are elections.

**dining room**
The household slaves are cleaning the house ready for a dinner party tonight.

**garden**
Most of the vegetables and herbs for the house are grown in the garden. The covered walkway is cool in summer but gets the sun in winter.

**Livia**
Titus's mother Livia is in charge of the house, and will spend the day making preparations for the dinner party. But before that she has to burn incense on the household shrine (*lararium*) to honour the gods that guard the house and the larder.

# In the street

Titus and his father set off for the temple of Jupiter. On the way, they stop at the bakery near their home to talk to Hermes, the owner. Titus munches on a pizza while his father and Hermes talk business. Hermes is a freedman, or freed slave. He used to be the cook at Titus's house, but then he bought his freedom from Titus's father.

**apartments**
Most people in Rome live in high-rise apartment blocks like this. The first-floor flats are large and roomy, but the top-floor flats are tiny, single rooms with no water or cooking facilities.

top-floor rooms

concrete

bricks

**apartment walls**
The walls of the apartment are made of concrete, covered with pyramid-shaped bricks pressed point-first into the wet concrete. The bricks are then covered with plaster.

first-floor apartment

**portico**
Fires are always breaking out in Rome. The emperor Augustus ruled that buildings had to have a walkway (portico) above street level to help firefighters get at fires.

aqueduct
bringing water
from the hills

**carts**
Carts are banned from the narrow streets during the day, unless they are carrying building supplies. This one is bringing wood for a damaged building.

Titus's
home

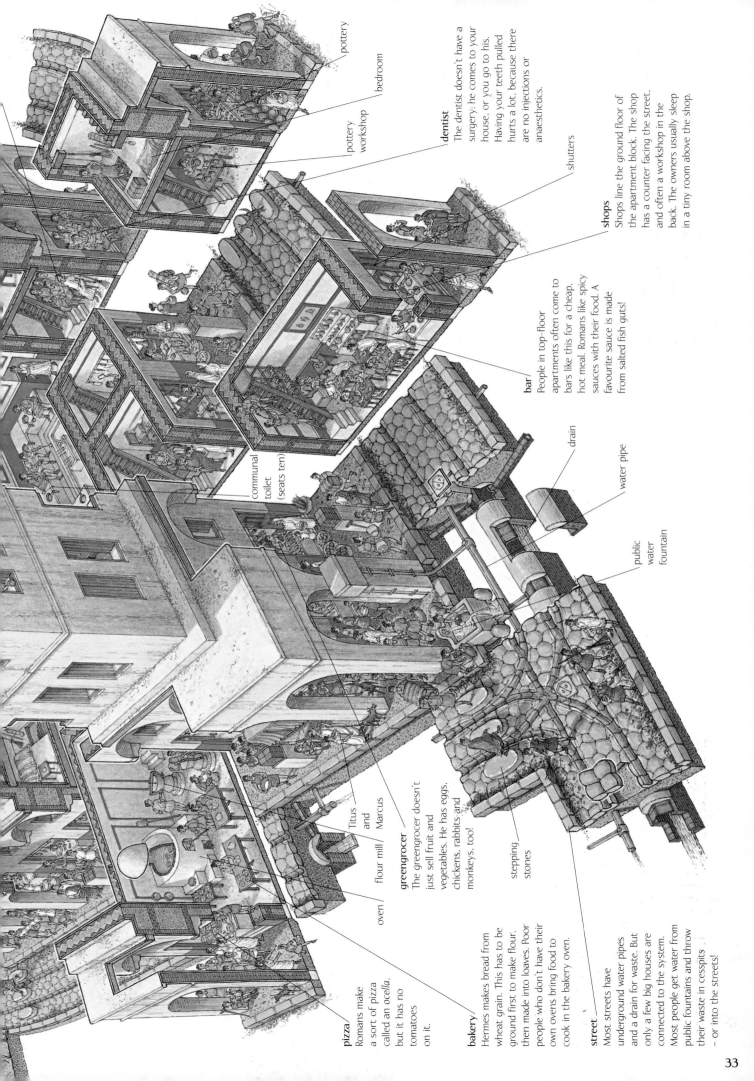

pottery

pottery
workshop

bedroom

**dentist**
The dentist doesn't have a surgery: he comes to your house, or you go to his. Having your teeth pulled hurts a lot, because there are no injections or anaesthetics.

shutters

**shops**
Shops line the ground floor of the apartment block. The shop has a counter facing the street, and often a workshop in the back. The owners usually sleep in a tiny room above the shop.

**bar**
People in top-floor apartments often come to bars like this for a cheap, hot meal. Romans like spicy sauces with their food. A favourite sauce is made from salted fish guts!

drain

water pipe

communal
toilet
(seats ten)

public
water
fountain

Titus
and
Marcus

**greengrocer**
The greengrocer doesn't just sell fruit and vegetables. He has eggs, chickens, rabbits and monkeys, too!

stepping
stones

oven    flour mill

**pizza**
Romans make a sort of pizza called an *ocella*, but it has no tomatoes on it.

**bakery**
Hermes makes bread from wheat grain. This has to be ground first to make flour, then made into loaves. Poor people who don't have their own ovens bring food to cook in the bakery oven.

**street**
Most streets have underground water pipes and a drain for waste. But only a few big houses are connected to the system. Most people get water from public fountains and throw their waste in cesspits – or into the streets!

33

# The Temple of Jupiter

There are lots of festival days each year, but Titus likes the festival of Castor and Pollux. Castor and Pollux are gods of horsemen, and so the procession includes hundreds of Roman cavalrymen. Titus loves watching the cavalrymen on their fine horses. They are wearing their best armour, and their shining bronze helmets and breastplates gleam in the sun. Titus and his father watch the horsemen pass, then join the procession.

## Temple

The Temple itself is very beautiful. The columns are milky white marble, while the roof and doors are covered in gold. Inside there are huge gold and ivory statues of three gods: Jupiter, Juno and Minerva.

## The ceremony

At the start of the ceremony the priest tosses incense into the altar flame and sprinkles wine and cakes on the altar. Next he offers up a prayer to Castor and Pollux. Now the animals are sacrificed. An official stuns each animal with a hammer, then another official kills it. Some of the meat from the sacrifices is burnt on the altar fires. Afterwards, the worshippers feast on the meat that is not burnt.

### The legend of Castor and Pollux

Hundreds of years ago, the Romans fought a battle against a group of enemies at Lake Regillus, south-east of Rome. The fight was going badly for the Romans, until two shining young men on white horses appeared and led them to victory. Later that day, the same men were seen watering their tired horses at a fountain in the Forum. They told the citizens about the victory at Lake Regillus and then disappeared. The temple of Castor and Pollux was built on the site of the fountain in the Forum.

statue

gold covering on tiles

bronze roof tiles

capital (top) of column

golden doors

Minerva

Jupiter

carving of gods

statue

Juno

marble columns made of smaller drums

marble drum

34

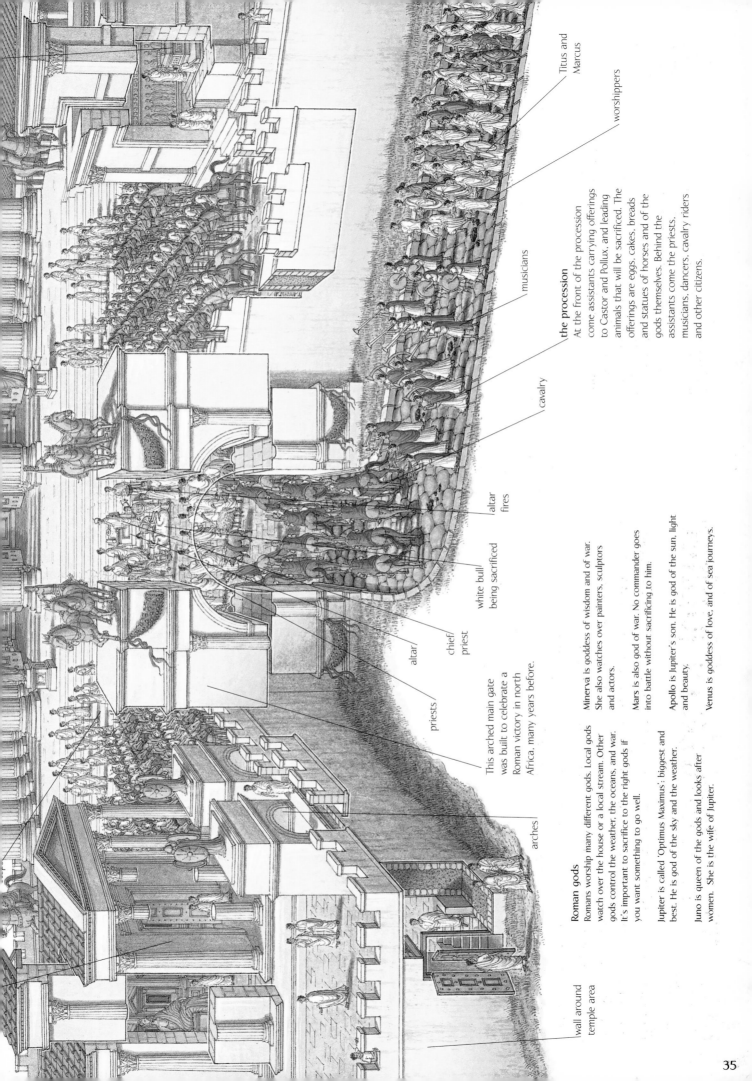

wall around temple area

arches

This arched main gate was built to celebrate a Roman victory in north Africa, many years before.

priests

altar

chief priest

white bull being sacrificed

altar fires

cavalry

musicians

Titus and Marcus

worshippers

### the procession

At the front of the procession come assistants carrying offerings to Castor and Pollux, and leading animals that will be sacrificed. The offerings are eggs, cakes, breads and statues of horses and of the gods themselves. Behind the assistants come the priests, musicians, dancers, cavalry riders and other citizens.

### Roman gods

Romans worship many different gods. Local gods watch over the house or a local stream. Other gods control the weather, the oceans, and war. It's important to sacrifice to the right gods if you want something to go well.

Jupiter is called 'Optimus Maximus': biggest and best. He is god of the sky and the weather.

Juno is queen of the gods and looks after women. She is the wife of Jupiter.

Minerva is goddess of wisdom and of war. She also watches over painters, sculptors and actors.

Mars is also god of war. No commander goes into battle without sacrificing to him.

Apollo is Jupiter's son. He is god of the sun, light and beauty.

Venus is goddess of love, and of sea journeys.

# The Forum Romanum

After the procession, Titus and his father head for the games at the Colosseum. On their way through the Forum Romanum, they meet another senator, called Antony. Marcus and Antony run a business together, bringing olive oil from Spain to Rome. Antony says that a ship has just arrived with a new cargo of olive oil. 'I'll go to the docks later to check the cargo,' says Marcus.

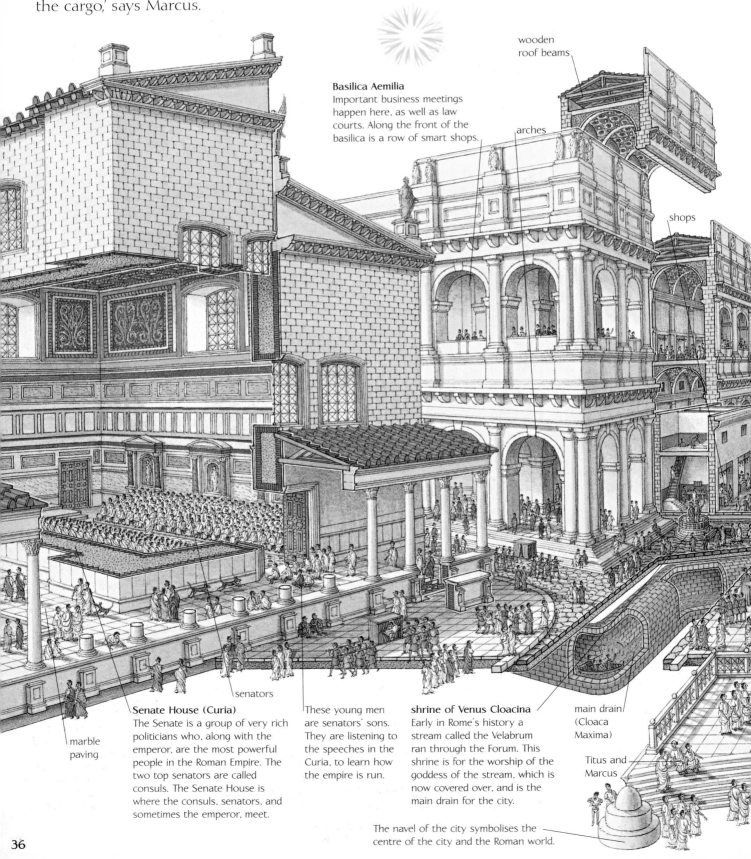

**Basilica Aemilia**
Important business meetings happen here, as well as law courts. Along the front of the basilica is a row of smart shops.

wooden roof beams

arches

shops

**Senate House (Curia)**
The Senate is a group of very rich politicians who, along with the emperor, are the most powerful people in the Roman Empire. The two top senators are called consuls. The Senate House is where the consuls, senators, and sometimes the emperor, meet.

senators

marble paving

These young men are senators' sons. They are listening to the speeches in the Curia, to learn how the empire is run.

**shrine of Venus Cloacina**
Early in Rome's history a stream called the Velabrum ran through the Forum. This shrine is for the worship of the goddess of the stream, which is now covered over, and is the main drain for the city.

main drain (Cloaca Maxima)

Titus and Marcus

The navel of the city symbolises the centre of the city and the Roman world.

## Citizens, freedmen and slaves

Everyone in Italy who is born free (not a slave) is a Roman citizen. This means that they can vote for government officials when there are elections.

The emperor is the most important citizen. The first emperor, Augustus, called himself 'first among equals'.

The consuls and senators are next in importance. They are all very rich and powerful.

The knights (equites) are rich citizens who have important jobs in the army and the government.

Ordinary citizens are much poorer than senators or knights. Many are shopkeepers or farmers.

Freedmen and women are freed slaves. They often become shopkeepers, too.

Slaves are mostly foreign prisoners who are bought and sold. Some have terrible jobs such as working in mines. But a few skilled slaves such as actors or cooks become rich and famous.

During the 4th hour (10.15 a.m.)

## Temple of Vesta

Vesta is the goddess of the hearth (home fire). Inside the Temple of Vesta is a holy fire, which is the 'hearth' for the whole city. The fire is kept alive day and night by a group of priestesses called the Vestal Virgins.

## Temple of Divus Julius

When the Roman leader Julius Caesar was killed, this temple was built in his honour. People began to worship him like a god. Augustus and other emperors who have died have temples and are worshipped as gods, too.

## Temple of Castor

The temple of Castor and Pollux is decorated in honour of the day's festival. The temple is a centre for banking, and also the office of weights and measures.

## Arch of Augustus

This arch was built by the Emperor Augustus to celebrate his victories in battle.

Important people sometimes travel in litters like this one.

People scratch game boards on these steps to play chequers and dice games.

nave

galleries

## Basilica Julia

Some of Rome's most important law courts are held in the Basilica Julia, and in the Basilica Aemilia opposite. The high space in the centre of the basilica is called the nave. Around it are galleries on two storeys.

pegs

ships' prows

## Speaker's platform

This Rostra is a platform for public speeches. Around the edges are the prows (fronts) of warships that the Romans captured in battle.

## Forum

The Forum is the centre of Rome. This is where Empire is governed from, and where the laws are made.

The golden milestone shows the distances to all the key cities of the Roman Empire.

peg holes

37

# The Colosseum

Titus is really looking forward to the games; he hasn't been to the Colosseum before. It's early, but the amphitheatre is already filled with a roaring crowd of thousands of people. The show starts with some amazing performing elephants. One draws letters in the sand with its foot. Next the hunters enter, each carrying only a spear. Snarling lions and leopards appear from nowhere, all round the hunters. The big cats attack…

**vomitoria**
There are 64 entrances (*vomitoria*) to the seating area. This means that if there is a fire or an emergency, everyone can get out quickly.

**concrete and brick**
The upper parts of the building are made of brick and concrete. Roman concrete is waterproof and strengthens with age.

**Colossus**
The Colossus gives the Colosseum its name. It is a statue of the sun-god, Helios, which is over 30 metres tall.

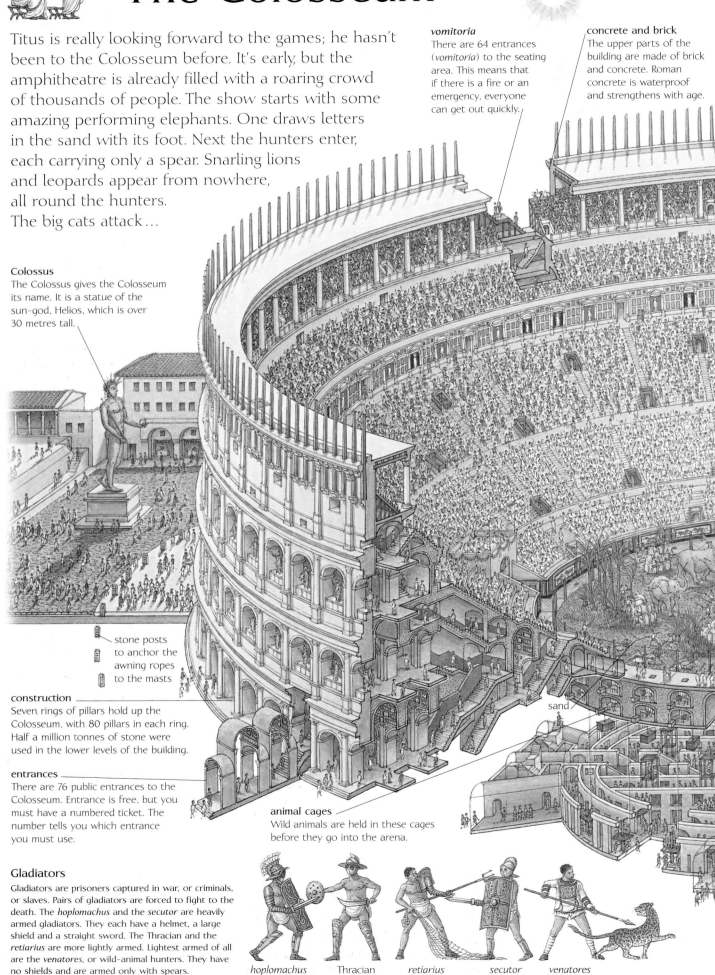

stone posts to anchor the awning ropes to the masts

**construction**
Seven rings of pillars hold up the Colosseum, with 80 pillars in each ring. Half a million tonnes of stone were used in the lower levels of the building.

**entrances**
There are 76 public entrances to the Colosseum. Entrance is free, but you must have a numbered ticket. The number tells you which entrance you must use.

sand

**animal cages**
Wild animals are held in these cages before they go into the arena.

## Gladiators

Gladiators are prisoners captured in war, or criminals, or slaves. Pairs of gladiators are forced to fight to the death. The *hoplomachus* and the *secutor* are heavily armed gladiators. They each have a helmet, a large shield and a straight sword. The Thracian and the *retiarius* are more lightly armed. Lightest armed of all are the *venatores*, or wild-animal hunters. They have no shields and are armed only with spears.

*hoplomachus*  Thracian  *retiarius*  *secutor*  *venatores*

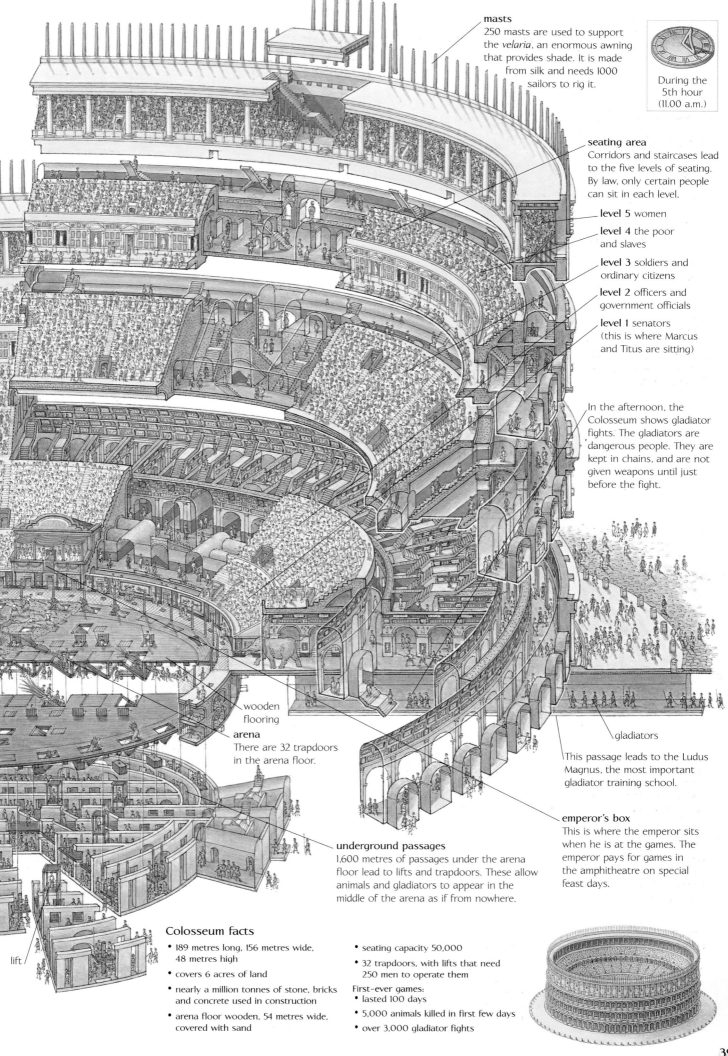

**masts**
250 masts are used to support the *velaria*, an enormous awning that provides shade. It is made from silk and needs 1000 sailors to rig it.

During the 5th hour (11.00 a.m.)

**seating area**
Corridors and staircases lead to the five levels of seating. By law, only certain people can sit in each level.

**level 5** women

**level 4** the poor and slaves

**level 3** soldiers and ordinary citizens

**level 2** officers and government officials

**level 1** senators (this is where Marcus and Titus are sitting)

In the afternoon, the Colosseum shows gladiator fights. The gladiators are dangerous people. They are kept in chains, and are not given weapons until just before the fight.

**gladiators**

This passage leads to the Ludus Magnus, the most important gladiator training school.

**emperor's box**
This is where the emperor sits when he is at the games. The emperor pays for games in the amphitheatre on special feast days.

**wooden flooring**

**arena**
There are 32 trapdoors in the arena floor.

**underground passages**
1,600 metres of passages under the arena floor lead to lifts and trapdoors. These allow animals and gladiators to appear in the middle of the arena as if from nowhere.

**lift**

## Colosseum facts

- 189 metres long, 156 metres wide, 48 metres high
- covers 6 acres of land
- nearly a million tonnes of stone, bricks and concrete used in construction
- arena floor wooden, 54 metres wide, covered with sand

- seating capacity 50,000
- 32 trapdoors, with lifts that need 250 men to operate them

First-ever games:
- lasted 100 days
- 5,000 animals killed in first few days
- over 3,000 gladiator fights

39

# At the docks

Titus's father has to go to the docks to check on his cargo of olive oil. Everyone at the docks is incredibly busy. Crane ropes creak, oxen bellow, and the air smells of wine, olives and sweaty bodies. Grumpy porters yell and jostle anyone who gets in their way. Oof! One of them bashes into Titus.

Titus's father talks to an official about his cargo. They go to make sure that the oil is good quality.

### Monte Testaccio ('hill of pots')

This hill is over 30 metres high, taller than four houses, and it's made entirely of broken pots! Used olive oil amphoras are dumped here, because they become smelly and can't be used again. Walls divide each level of the hill into small areas, to stop the whole thing from collapsing. The pots are covered with lime to stop them smelling.

### Goods from around the world

A city of over a million people takes a lot of feeding! Every day, merchants bring in many tonnes of food and other goods from all over the known world. There is wheat, building stone and papyrus from Egypt, wine from Greece and Gaul, wool, pottery and perfumes from Syria and Arabia, wood and horses from Dacia (Eastern Europe), wild animals from north Africa, gold, copper, oil and wine from Spain, and wool, tin and iron from Britannia (Britain).

Large ships bringing food and other cargoes cannot get up the river Tiber, so they unload at the port of Ostia on the coast. The ship's cargo is then loaded into barges and pulled up the river by teams of oxen.

towpath

team of oxen

empty barges returning to Ostia

River Tiber

← To Ostia

shelving for amphoras

vaulted (arched) ceiling

sacks of grain

wool

donkeys carrying amphoras

'tugboats' help to moor the barges

stone

mooring rings

crane

wine

porters

**warehouse**
The warehouse covers as much ground as five football pitches, and there are 200 storerooms. From here, the goods will be moved to smaller warehouses in different parts of the city.

flat roof

dividing walls

supporting pillars

silk

wine

**cranes**
These cranes can lift up to 7000 kg – the weight of a really big elephant. Sometimes they are used to lift real elephants brought in for the games!

cranes powered by slaves walking in a treadmill

Titus

**amphoras**
These big jars are called amphoras. They are used to carry wine, oil, honey, and a spicy, smelly fish sauce called garum that Romans love.

storeroom

olive oil

broken amphora

Marcus

**porters**
Once on the dock, hundreds of porters carry the sacks, barrels and amphoras to the warehouse. Merchants hire storerooms in the warehouse where they can store their goods.

**barges**
A flat-bottomed boat called a *caudicaria navis* carries cargoes up the river Tiber from Ostia. The barges are about 14 metres long and 5 metres wide.

To Rome ➤

## Goods brought to Rome by river

perfumes from Arabia

grain from Egypt

pottery from Syria

ivory from east Africa

oil from Spain

wood from Cyrenica (north Africa)

hides from Germania (Germany)

silk from China

wool from Britannia

horses from Dacia (Eastern Europe)

wine from Gaul (France)

wild animals from Mauretania (north Africa)

# The Baths of Trajan

After the dock visit, Titus and his father go to relax and wash at the baths. They meet lots of friends there. Titus swims while his father plays ball and has a massage. Then they soak in the hot tub before taking a refreshing plunge in the cold pool. Titus's father buys them both a drink before they leave.

All Romans enjoy coming to the baths. It is not just a place to wash. People exercise, have a massage, talk business, have a bite to eat, go for a walk, read, or just relax and chat with friends. Women and men usually bathe at different times, women in the morning and men in the mid-afternoon.

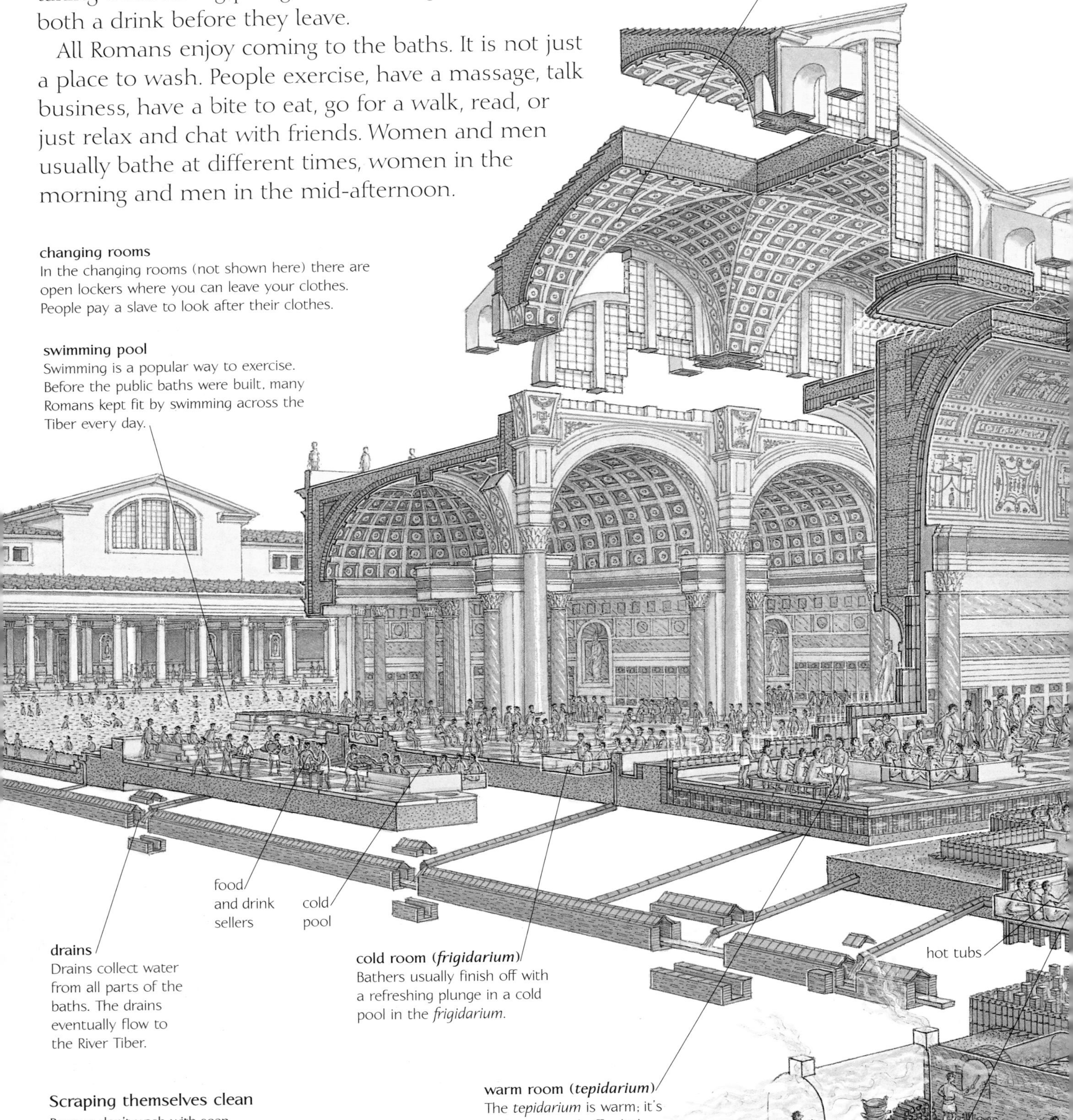

**changing rooms**
In the changing rooms (not shown here) there are open lockers where you can leave your clothes. People pay a slave to look after their clothes.

**swimming pool**
Swimming is a popular way to exercise. Before the public baths were built, many Romans kept fit by swimming across the Tiber every day.

**ceiling**
The vaulted (arched) ceiling is made of concrete. The square decorations are called coffers, and they help give the ceiling strength.

food and drink sellers

cold pool

**drains**
Drains collect water from all parts of the baths. The drains eventually flow to the River Tiber.

**cold room (*frigidarium*)**
Bathers usually finish off with a refreshing plunge in a cold pool in the *frigidarium*.

hot tubs

**Scraping themselves clean**
Romans don't wash with soap. First, they exercise or sunbathe to get themselves sweaty. Then they get a slave attendant to rub their skin with oil. Finally the slave scrapes off the oil and dirt using a scraper called a strigil.

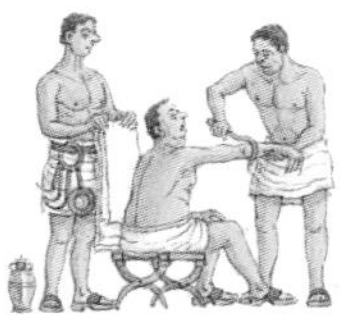

**warm room (*tepidarium*)**
The *tepidarium* is warm; it's a place to cool off a little after the *caldarium*.

**hot room (*caldarium*)**
People start by relaxing in steaming hot water tubs in the hot room (*caldarium*).

**roof spaces**
Air spaces in the roof eventually carry warm air from the baths to the outside.

warm air escaping

**hollow walls**
The walls of the warm and hot rooms also have hollow walls. Warm air from the hypocaust rises up through these spaces.

**windows**
The sun shines in through huge, south-facing windows to help heat up the warm and hot rooms.

**exercise yard**
There is also an exercise yard. Some people play ball or wrestle to work up a sweat, while others just sunbathe.

hot water tank

**heating system (hypocaust)**
The furnace room also heats air for the hypocaust. This is a system of tunnels that carries hot air under the floor of the warm and hot rooms.

**water pipes**
The water for Trajan's Baths comes in pipes from two different aqueducts. Some water comes straight to the baths, but some is stored in a reservoir called the Sette Sale.

fuel basket

**furnaces**
Below the bathing rooms there is a furnace room. The furnaces heat two water tanks, which fill the hot tubs in the *caldarium*. Water from the tanks is also mixed with cold water for the warm pools in the *tepidarium*.

nace
om

43

# At the races

The best treat of the day is the chariot races at the Circus Maximus. Everyone is shouting for their favourite team. Titus and his father support the Green team. 'Come on Greens!', Titus yells. But on the first turn a Red charioteer swings round too tightly and his chariot turns over – right in the path of one of the Green chariots. Luckily, the drivers are unhurt. They struggle to cut their horses free before the chariots come round again.

**Circus Maximus**
The Circus Maximus is the biggest stadium ever! It is 600 metres long – bigger than any modern sports or football stadium. It holds 250,000 people. The Circus was first laid out by Rome's King Tarquin, in about 500 B.C.

**starting gates**
The starting gates have separate boxes for each chariot. A trumpet sounds to start the race. A clever mechanism makes all twelve gates spring open at once, and the chariots charge out.

**spina**
The *spina* runs down the middle of the circus, like the central reservation on a motorway. Three pillars at either end mark the turning points.

starting boxes

spring-operated starting gates

dolphins

**water pools**
Each team has a water pool on the *spina*. As their chariots go past, slaves throw water over the sweating horses.

**chariot teams**
Each chariot and charioteer belongs to one of four teams: Reds, Whites, Greens or Blues. There are twelve chariots in the race, three from each team. These chariots are *quadrigas*: four-horse teams.

**betting**
All through the crowd, people are betting on who will win the race. Roman law says that betting is illegal, but no one seems to mind!

snack-seller

Titus and Marcus

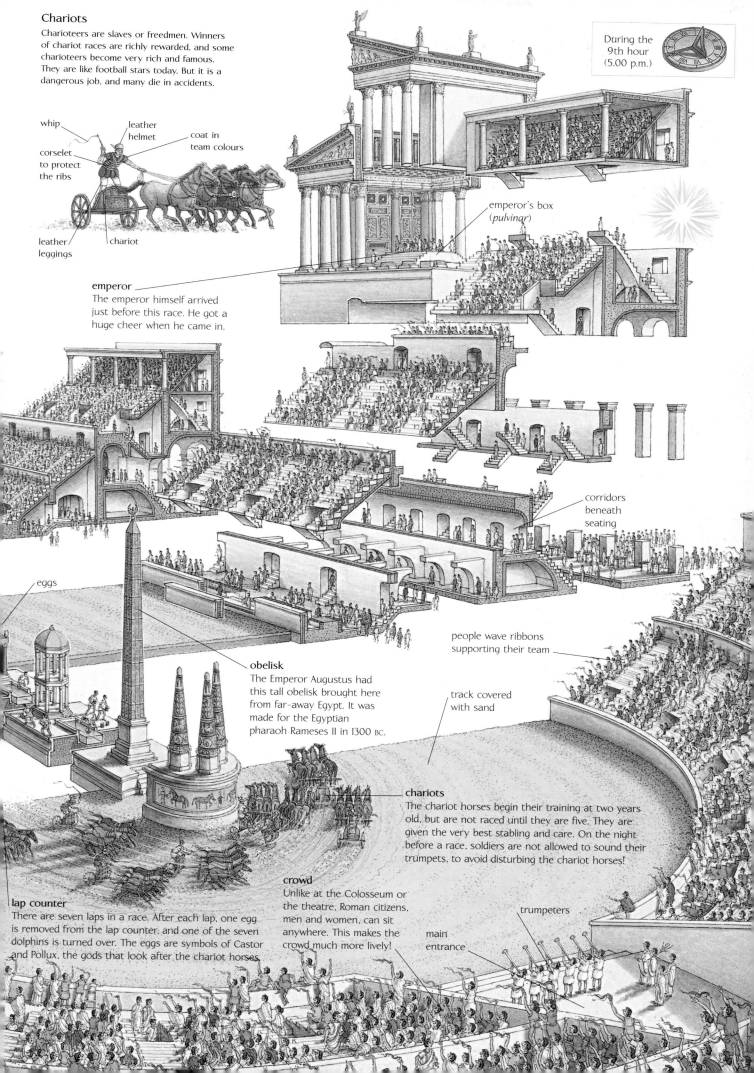

## Chariots

Charioteers are slaves or freedmen. Winners of chariot races are richly rewarded, and some charioteers become very rich and famous. They are like football stars today. But it is a dangerous job, and many die in accidents.

whip
leather helmet
corselet to protect the ribs
coat in team colours
leather leggings
chariot

During the 9th hour (5.00 p.m.)

emperor's box (*pulvinar*)

**emperor**
The emperor himself arrived just before this race. He got a huge cheer when he came in.

corridors beneath seating

**eggs**

**obelisk**
The Emperor Augustus had this tall obelisk brought here from far-away Egypt. It was made for the Egyptian pharaoh Rameses II in 1300 BC.

people wave ribbons supporting their team

track covered with sand

**chariots**
The chariot horses begin their training at two years old, but are not raced until they are five. They are given the very best stabling and care. On the night before a race, soldiers are not allowed to sound their trumpets, to avoid disturbing the chariot horses!

**lap counter**
There are seven laps in a race. After each lap, one egg is removed from the lap counter, and one of the seven dolphins is turned over. The eggs are symbols of Castor and Pollux, the gods that look after the chariot horses.

**crowd**
Unlike at the Colosseum or the theatre, Roman citizens, men and women, can sit anywhere. This makes the crowd much more lively!

main entrance

trumpeters

# Home again

When Titus and his father get back from the chariot racing, it's time for supper. Titus eats in the kitchen. He is too young to go to the grown-ups' feast.

Before Titus goes to bed, his father comes in with a package. 'I got this for you at the Colosseum,' he says. It's a model gladiator!

**Food**

On normal days the family eats simple food, such as bread, cheese, vegetables, olives and a little meat. At a dinner party the food is rich and spicy. Romans like spicy sauces with their food. A favourite one is *garum*, or *liquamen*, which is made from fish that have been left to rot in the sun for several days!

**doorkeeper**
The doorkeeper bars the house door, and brings the guard dog from its kennel.

guard dog

**street**
At night the streets are noisy and dangerous. There are no street lights, so it's very dark. Huge carts constantly rumble up and down the streets, and there are thieves waiting to pounce on people.

**shops**
The bronzesmith is closing up his shop for the night. He covers the front with large shutters.

**nightwatchmen**
A band of nightwatchmen patrol the streets. They try to stop robbers and other criminals, but there aren't really enough of them to make the streets safe.

**Titus's bedroom**
Titus lies in bed with his model gladiator, and listens to the music and laughter from the dining room. He is beginning to feel very sleepy.

torchbearer

chamber pot

litter

**Fulvia's room**
Baby Fulvia is already asleep. The wet nurse dozes in a chair by the cradle.

POLYBIUM AED O.V.F.

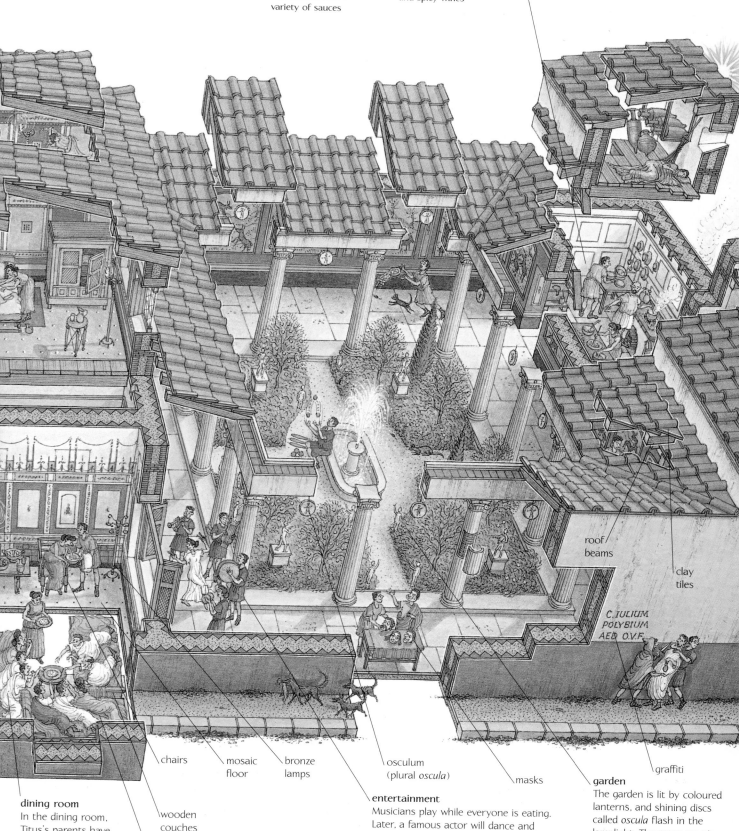

## MENU

**gustatio (appetizers)**
- eggs
- salads
- radishes
- mushrooms
- olives
- oysters
- bread rolls

**prima mensa (main meal)**
- a roasted pig
- boiled pig's udders
- fried chicken with leeks
- boiled veal (calf)
- pigeons
- snails fattened on milk
- sea mussels
- tuna
– all served with a variety of sauces

**secunda mensa – dessert**
- pear soufflé
- pancakes with milk
- pastries
- fresh fruit
- nuts

**To drink**
- a selection of sweet and spicy wines

**kitchen**
The slaves in the kitchen are still busy setting out food on dishes. Chilo is already cross because his best helper is ill in bed. Now his replacement has just dropped a whole tray of pastries!

During the 11th hour (8.00 p.m.)

roof beams

clay tiles

C. IULIUM POLYBIUM AED O.V.F.

chairs

mosaic floor

bronze lamps

osculum (plural *oscula*)

masks

graffiti

**garden**
The garden is lit by coloured lanterns, and shining discs called *oscula* flash in the lamplight. The actor practises with his masks while he waits to entertain the guests.

**dining room**
In the dining room, Titus's parents have guests for dinner. The men and women eat lying on couches, or sitting on chairs.

wooden couches

cloths and cushions

**entertainment**
Musicians play while everyone is eating. Later, a famous actor will dance and perform a funny play for the guests. There is sweet and spicy wine with the meal, but after dessert the men will drink more wine and talk until late in the night.

# GREECE

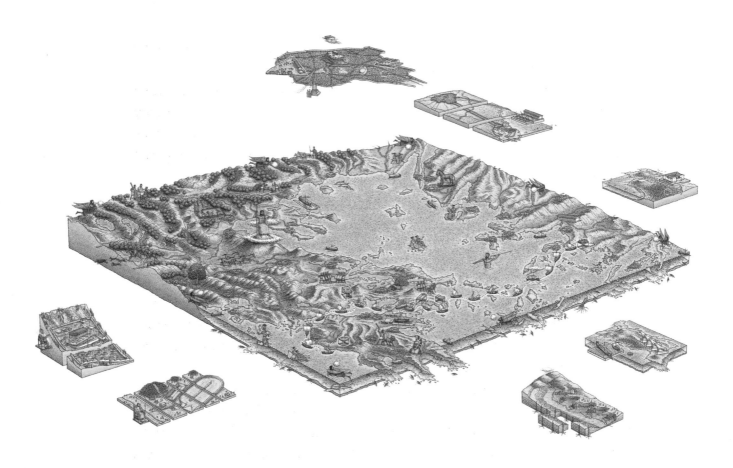

# 'Why I am proud to be a Greek'
## by Neleus, son of Aristagoras the Milesian

Aristagoras
Mother
Penelope
Neleus
Helen
Peri
*paidagogos*

I am proud to be a Greek because we are the world's most civilized and powerful people. Three things show this.

First, we dwell with the gods: on Mount Olympus in the Greek state of Thessaly live Zeus, king of the gods, and eleven other mighty deities. Such neighbours are the greatest honour, but they are easily angered and we have to take care not to annoy them. Everything that goes wrong is a punishment from the gods for our folly.

Second, our way of life is the best. We are organized into prosperous, well-run states, each with its own capital city and surrounding countryside. Athens, the richest and grandest city-state, has overseas settlements and allies like Miletus, where we live. Sparta, Athens' rival, is a famous military power. All Greeks share the same wonderful language, with its rich traditions of poetry, philosophy and history. We are great thinkers: who else knows as much about government, science and astronomy? We use silver money, too, and hold fantastic athletic games.

Third, we proved our greatness when we defeated the invading Persians. The first Greek triumph was when the Athenians and Plataeans smashed the enemy at Marathon. The Spartans led by Leonidas then brilliantly held up their advance at Thermopylae. Finally, the Athenian fleet won a great victory at Salamis and the Persian army was overwhelmed at Plataea. The fighting ended about thirty years ago.

The only thing that might damage our wonderful civilization is if we fight amongst ourselves. This did happen a while back, when Athens and Sparta fell out. Today we are still enjoying the fruits of the thirty-year truce they made just after I was born.

# Our journey

I'm Neleus, aged almost 12, and I've just returned from the fantastic journey shown on this map. My father, the grain merchant Aristagoras, took me and my younger brother Periander ('Peri', who is 10) to Athens. Dad had important business to sort out there. We then sailed to Delphi, where we consulted the world-famous oracle. Finally, the gods decided our family's future in a wrestling match at the Olympic Games.
Cool trip, eh?

**DAY 32**

**The theatre of Dionysus**
This famous theatre nestles beneath the city's Acropolis. on which stands the mighty Parthenon, the temple of Athene.

**DAY 29**

**The Agora at Athens**
The open space at the heart of the city, surrounded by important public buildings, commonly serves as a market place.

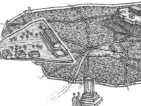

**Artemis**
The virgin deity Artemis was the goddess of hunting, animals and childbirth. Her temple at Ephesus was one of the Seven Wonders of the ancient world.

Zeus on Mount Olympus

woodcutters near Amphipolis, a vital Greek frontier post

Boreas, the north wind

canal dug through the Athos peninsular by the Persian king Xerxes

shepherd with his flock

lion mosaic at Pella, capital of Macedonia

mountain bandits

Tricca, famous for its fine horses

AEGEAN SEA

trire

hunting

Dodona, site of an oracle of Zeus

Zeus' sacred oak at Dodona, founded as a sanctuary by a black dove

Zephyrus, the west wind

Thermopylae

Ithaca, birthplace of Odysseus, hero of Homer's *Odyssey*

**DAY 50**

**Delphi**
The temple of Apollo, from which the god issues his famous prophetic utterances, is on the southern slopes of Mount Parnassus.

**DAY 71**

**Olympia**
Here the greatest of all athletic games have been held in honour of Zeus every four years for 340 years.

**Heracles in Nemea**
Made mad by the goddess Hera, the Greek hero Heracles (the Roman Hercules) killed his own children. As a punishment he had to perform 12 near-impossible labours. He began by strangling the invulnerable Nemean Lion.

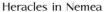

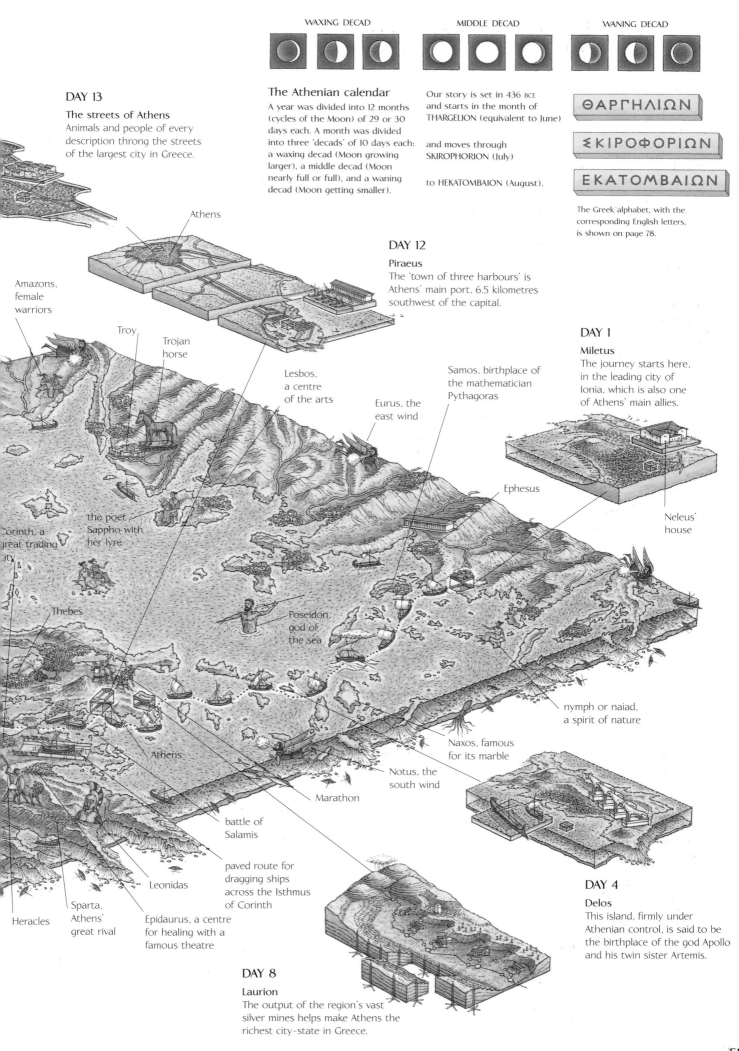

WAXING DECAD   MIDDLE DECAD   WANING DECAD

## DAY 13

### The streets of Athens
Animals and people of every description throng the streets of the largest city in Greece.

### The Athenian calendar
A year was divided into 12 months (cycles of the Moon) of 29 or 30 days each. A month was divided into three 'decads' of 10 days each: a waxing decad (Moon growing larger), a middle decad (Moon nearly full or full), and a waning decad (Moon getting smaller).

Our story is set in 436 BCE and starts in the month of THARGELION (equivalent to June)

and moves through SKIROPHORION (July)

to HEKATOMBAION (August).

ΘΑΡΓΗΛΙΩΝ

ΣΚΙΡΟΦΟΡΙΩΝ

ΕΚΑΤΟΜΒΑΙΩΝ

The Greek alphabet, with the corresponding English letters, is shown on page 78.

## DAY 12

### Piraeus
The 'town of three harbours' is Athens' main port, 6.5 kilometres southwest of the capital.

## DAY 1

### Miletus
The journey starts here, in the leading city of Ionia, which is also one of Athens' main allies.

Athens

Amazons, female warriors

Troy

Trojan horse

Lesbos, a centre of the arts

Samos, birthplace of the mathematician Pythagoras

Eurus, the east wind

Ephesus

Neleus' house

the poet Sappho with her lyre

Corinth, a great trading city

Poseidon, god of the sea

nymph or naiad, a spirit of nature

Thebes

Naxos, famous for its marble

Notus, the south wind

Athens

Marathon

battle of Salamis

paved route for dragging ships across the Isthmus of Corinth

## DAY 4

### Delos
This island, firmly under Athenian control, is said to be the birthplace of the god Apollo and his twin sister Artemis.

Leonidas

Sparta, Athens' great rival

Epidaurus, a centre for healing with a famous theatre

Heracles

## DAY 8

### Laurion
The output of the region's vast silver mines helps make Athens the richest city-state in Greece.

# At home in Miletus

We didn't sleep much the night before we left. Dad had a noisy farewell party – he was in a good mood because he'd just heard from Aspasia. She's the Milesian girlfriend of Pericles, a really important Athenian politician. Her letter said Pericles would help dad in the Athenian courts. After packing, Peri and I argued for hours about the Milesian wrestler Thrasyboulos. Peri reckoned 'Boulos' was certain to win the Olympics. I wasn't so sure.

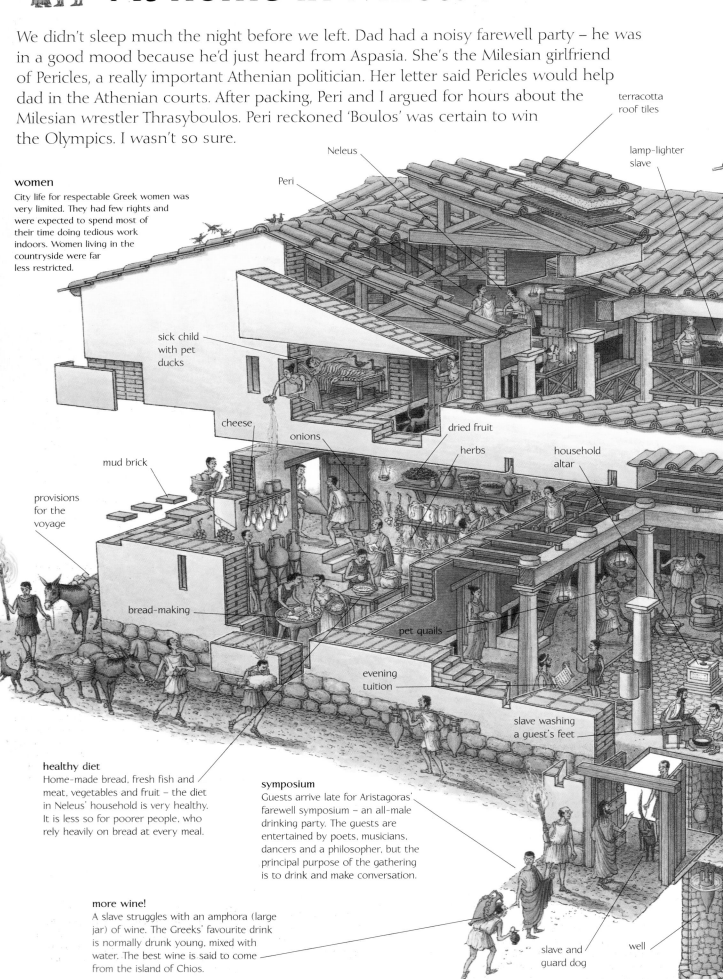

**women**
City life for respectable Greek women was very limited. They had few rights and were expected to spend most of their time doing tedious work indoors. Women living in the countryside were far less restricted.

terracotta roof tiles

lamp-lighter slave

Neleus

Peri

sick child with pet ducks

cheese

mud brick

onions

dried fruit

herbs

household altar

provisions for the voyage

bread-making

pet quails

evening tuition

slave washing a guest's feet

**healthy diet**
Home-made bread, fresh fish and meat, vegetables and fruit – the diet in Neleus' household is very healthy. It is less so for poorer people, who rely heavily on bread at every meal.

**symposium**
Guests arrive late for Aristagoras' farewell symposium – an all-male drinking party. The guests are entertained by poets, musicians, dancers and a philosopher, but the principal purpose of the gathering is to drink and make conversation.

**more wine!**
A slave struggles with an amphora (large jar) of wine. The Greeks' favourite drink is normally drunk young, mixed with water. The best wine is said to come from the island of Chios.

slave and guard dog

well

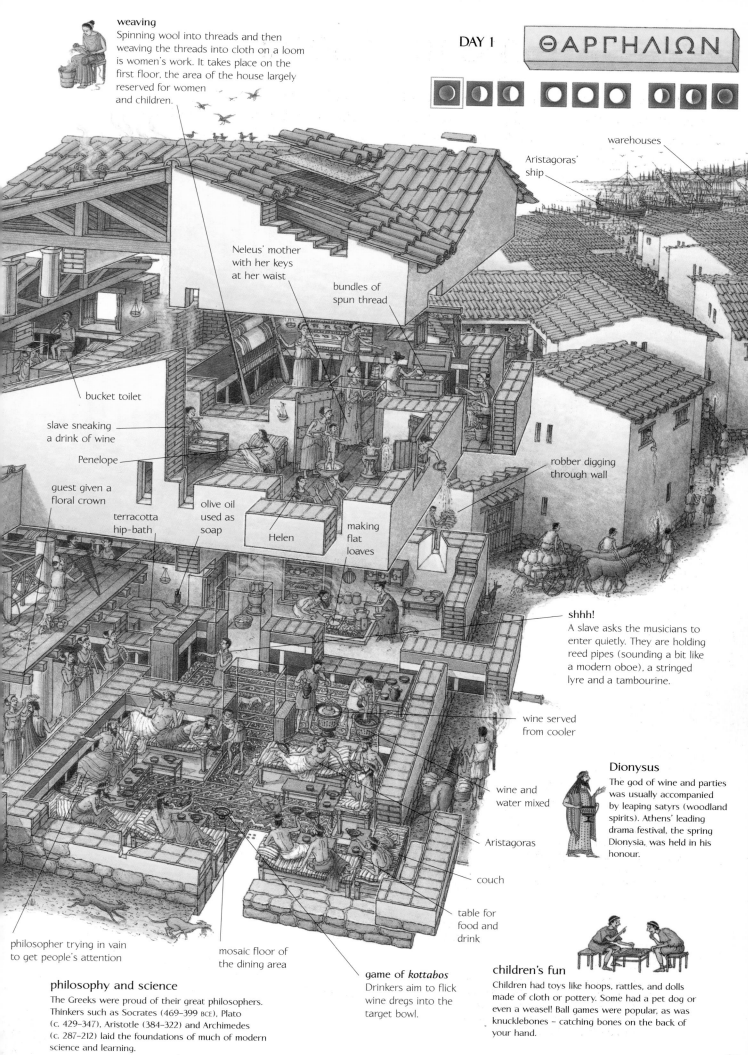

**weaving**
Spinning wool into threads and then weaving the threads into cloth on a loom is women's work. It takes place on the first floor, the area of the house largely reserved for women and children.

warehouses

Aristagoras' ship

Neleus' mother with her keys at her waist

bundles of spun thread

bucket toilet

slave sneaking a drink of wine

Penelope

robber digging through wall

guest given a floral crown

terracotta hip-bath

olive oil used as soap

Helen

making flat loaves

**shhh!**
A slave asks the musicians to enter quietly. They are holding reed pipes (sounding a bit like a modern oboe), a stringed lyre and a tambourine.

wine served from cooler

**Dionysus**
The god of wine and parties was usually accompanied by leaping satyrs (woodland spirits). Athens' leading drama festival, the spring Dionysia, was held in his honour.

wine and water mixed

Aristagoras

couch

table for food and drink

philosopher trying in vain to get people's attention

mosaic floor of the dining area

**game of *kottabos***
Drinkers aim to flick wine dregs into the target bowl.

**children's fun**
Children had toys like hoops, rattles, and dolls made of cloth or pottery. Some had a pet dog or even a weasel! Ball games were popular, as was knucklebones – catching bones on the back of your hand.

**philosophy and science**
The Greeks were proud of their great philosophers. Thinkers such as Socrates (469–399 BCE), Plato (c. 429–347), Aristotle (384–322) and Archimedes (c. 287–212) laid the foundations of much of modern science and learning.

# Entering the harbour at Delos

After saying goodbye to mum and our sisters, we left in one of dad's cargo boats. We sailed by day, moving from island to island. On the second morning we hit a storm and I was horribly seasick. Peri just laughed. Later, entering Delos harbour, we passed an amazing sacred Athenian warship. Peri and I waved, but dad only muttered grumpily that it had probably been paid for by tribute collected from hard-up Milesians.

### Poseidon

The trident-wielding Poseidon, one of Zeus' brothers, ruled the kingdom of the seas. The Athenians held him in great respect because of their seafaring traditions and because he may have been father of their local hero Theseus.

slave transport ship

leather curtain

ship's sponsor

captain at the helm

mast

hoplite

priest

rowing master

yard and sail

owl
A shield decorated with an owl is associated with the wise, 'owl-eyed' goddess Athene after whom Athens is named.

shipwright making repairs

edge-to-edge planks

bailing

oak keel

### seafaring

Ships and the sea, important to most Greeks, were vital to Athenians. Their wealth came mostly from overseas trade and tribute, and their powerful navy was a mighty weapon for attack and defence.

### fishing

The Greeks ate vast quantities of fish and even imported extra supplies from the Black Sea. Fish was eaten fresh or preserved by salting or drying.

octopus     squid     tuna     mackerel

## Ares

Ares, the bloody, merciless yet sometimes cowardly god of war, was hated by his parents, Zeus and Hera. He had only one admirer, Hades, ruler of the Underworld, as Ares' antics helped populate his kingdom of dead souls.

Error

Error

 Scythian archer

thick rope to keep hull from sagging

greased leather cushion

## rowers

Athenian men work the triremes (warships) as part of their military service. A trireme is powered by 170 oarsmen, 85 on each side in three tiers. The shape of the oars is different on each tier.

## trireme

This special kind of ship is built of lighter wood on a heavy oak keel. The simple design allows Athens to build up to 200 ships a year.

eye motif

Error

 lead sheeting on hull

bronze ram

Error

Error

Error

Error

## Delos

The sacred island of Delos gave its name to a league dedicated to resisting the Persians. The league – and Delos – soon came under strong Athenian control. In 426 BCE Athens ordered that no one was to die or be born on the island.

storm damage

temple

Delos town

Peri

Neleus

*paidagogos*

Aristagoras

captain

steering oar

## settlements and colonies

The defeat of the Persians left Athens controlling a network of city-states around the Aegean Sea. Greeks also settled further afield, from Massilia in what is now southern France to Tell Sukas in Syria.

## pricey wood

Timber is scarce in southern Greece, making a wooden trireme a highly expensive piece of military equipment. Only Athens, with its rich silver mines and plentiful tribute, can afford to buy enough wood to build a large fleet.

## sea spear

36 metres long, 5.5 metres wide and capable of a maximum speed of about 18 kilometres an hour, a trireme was designed to skim over the water and pierce an enemy ship below the waterline with its deadly ram.

# The silver mines at Laurion

At Thorikos we stayed with one of dad's business friends. Dad explained that he was going to Athens because his agent there, Lyrias, had been stealing his money. Our host reckoned the Athenians had enough money without taking dad's. He showed us what he meant by giving us a tour of Athens' huge silver mine at Laurion. When Peri started messing about and fell into a tank, it was my turn to laugh!

**Hera**
After being rescued from the tank, Peri gave thanks to Hera. The sister-wife of Zeus and queen of the gods, Hera was the guardian of women, the home and children. She could be cruel, though, particularly towards her husband's girlfriends.

slag heap

sorting ore

ventilation shaft

fire to create ventilation draft

pounding ore into chippings

milling chippings into powder

dead slave

**oil lamp**
Oil lamps burn olive oil, one of the many uses the Greeks make of the precious olive tree that was Athene's gift to Athens.

ladder

rock pillar

**slavery**
In Greece, as in all ancient societies, slavery was regarded as normal. Slaves were seen as objects, not people, and their owners could do more or less what they wanted with them.

ore removed from workface

seam of silver ore 80 metres below ground

children breaking up ore

**mine slave**
Appalling working conditions mean that mine slaves (usually prisoners of war) rarely survive more than a year or two. Consequently, they have to be carefully guarded in case they try to rebel or escape.

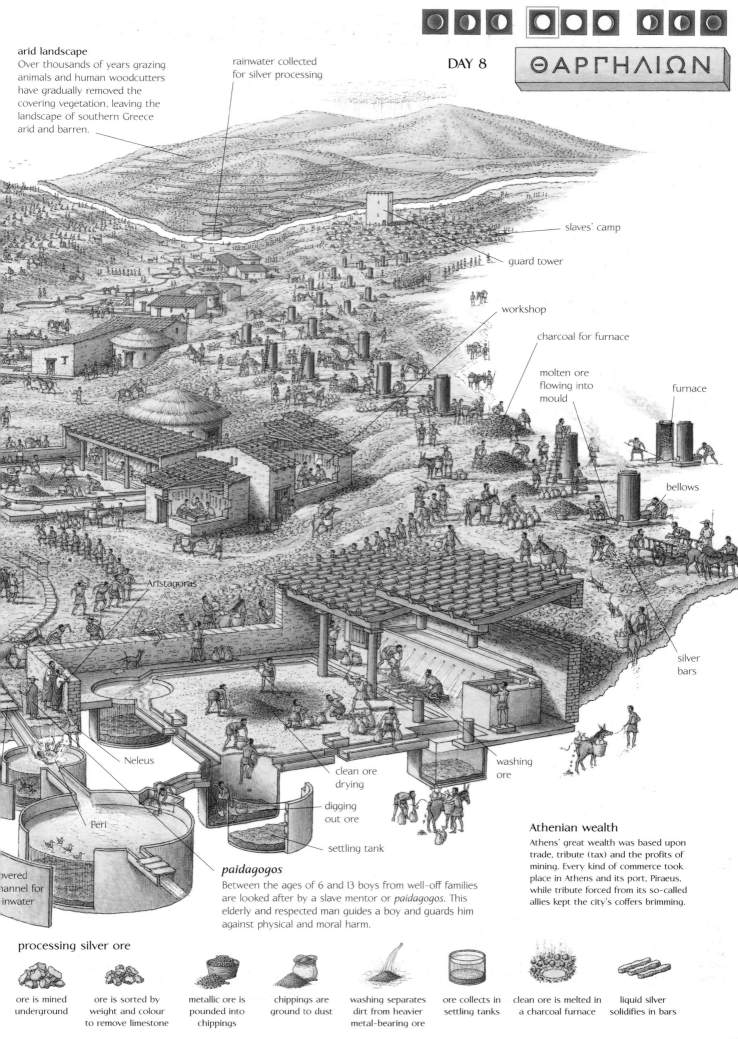

**arid landscape**
Over thousands of years grazing animals and human woodcutters have gradually removed the covering vegetation, leaving the landscape of southern Greece arid and barren.

rainwater collected for silver processing

slaves' camp

guard tower

workshop

charcoal for furnace

molten ore flowing into mould

furnace

bellows

silver bars

Aristagoras

Neleus

clean ore drying

digging out ore

settling tank

washing ore

Peri

covered channel for rainwater

*paidagogos*
Between the ages of 6 and 13 boys from well-off families are looked after by a slave mentor or *paidagogos*. This elderly and respected man guides a boy and guards him against physical and moral harm.

**Athenian wealth**
Athens' great wealth was based upon trade, tribute (tax) and the profits of mining. Every kind of commerce took place in Athens and its port, Piraeus, while tribute forced from its so-called allies kept the city's coffers brimming.

### processing silver ore

| ore is mined underground | ore is sorted by weight and colour to remove limestone | metallic ore is pounded into chippings | chippings are ground to dust | washing separates dirt from heavier metal-bearing ore | ore collects in settling tanks | clean ore is melted in a charcoal furnace | liquid silver solidifies in bars |

# Piraeus, the port of Athens

We finally reached Piraeus, the port of the city of Athens. I'd never dreamed of so many ships and so much cargo! That morning Peri had said he wanted to be a wrestler, like Boulos, and I'd said he was far too clumsy. My point was proved when, as dad was changing money, Peri knocked over a jar of really expensive wine. The owner made dad pay, which turned him even more anti-Athens.

**naval dockyard**
Athens' triremes would quickly become waterlogged if they remained at sea for long. Consequently, a huge naval dockyard is needed to store and repair them.

sail loft

arsenal for storing trireme equipment

warehouse

ox cart

rainwater spout

banking table

official set of weights and measures

Neleus

Peri in trouble

iron ingots

almonds

bales of cloth

rope

shields

Aristagoras

millstones

raisins

**metic businessman**
Metics are Greeks who have come to live in Athens and do business there. Their skill and hard work have helped to build the city's prosperity, although they have no say in the government and cannot own property.

**coinage**
Coins were invented in Lydia (in present-day Turkey) and adopted by the Greeks in the 6th century BCE. Athens' owl-stamped coins, handmade from the silver of Laurion, were of the highest quality.

## imports

As the territory around Athens (Attica) did not provide sufficient produce to feed the city, tonnes of grain were imported each year. There was also a ready market for luxuries like ivory, gold, silver, silk and perfumes.

## exports

Goods made in Athens were in demand right across the Mediterranean. Most popular were earthenware jars (amphoras) of wine, fine pottery, and a variety of items fashioned from iron or bronze.

## citizenship

Citizens were those born into families that had lived in and around Athens since the city's foundation. All male citizens took part in government and had to do military service. Women and children had few rights and were under the protection of their male relatives.

## Demeter

The mystical goddess of corn and all fruits of the earth, Demeter was also closely linked to the Underworld: her daughter Persephone was married to the grim lord Hades.

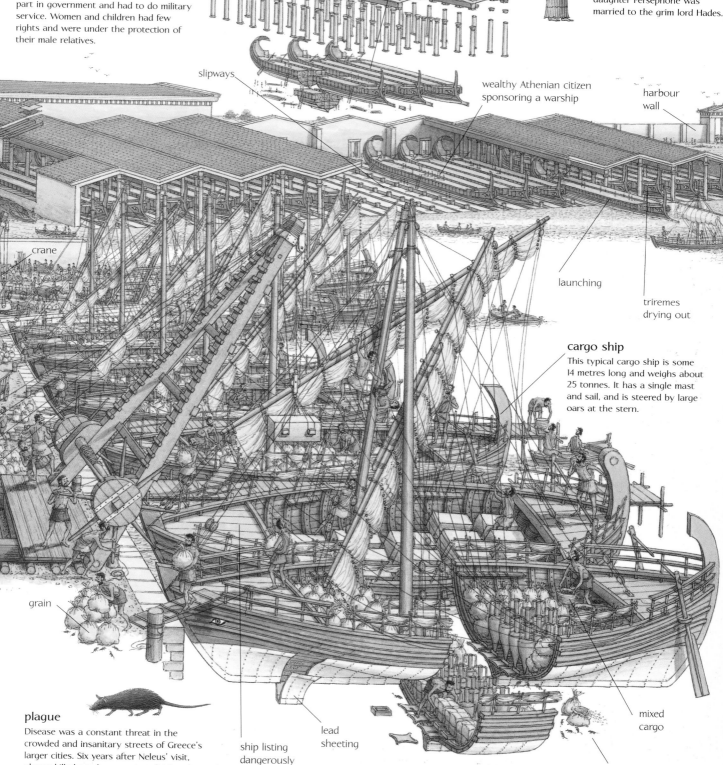

ship-building

trireme sheds

slipways

wealthy Athenian citizen sponsoring a warship

harbour wall

crane

launching

triremes drying out

## cargo ship

This typical cargo ship is some 14 metres long and weighs about 25 tonnes. It has a single mast and sail, and is steered by large oars at the stern.

grain

mixed cargo

## plague

Disease was a constant threat in the crowded and insanitary streets of Greece's larger cities. Six years after Neleus' visit, plague killed nearly a quarter of Athens' population. It was probably brought to the city by rats coming ashore at Piraeus.

ship listing dangerously

lead sheeting

rats

# Through Athens' crowded streets

I was disappointed with Athens. The greatest city in the world had majestic buildings and noble-looking people, of course, but there was too much foul-smelling dirt for my liking – and too many shady characters lurking in dark corners. To save money we stayed at a friend's house. Dad met with Aspasia and some experts on the law, and they worked together on his case. If he didn't win, our visit to Olympia would be cancelled.

### Aspasia

Miletus-born Aspasia was the girlfriend of Pericles, one of Athens' greatest leaders. She lived in Athens from about 440 BCE. Unlike most Greek women, she was well educated and able to match the intellectual skills of men.

### teacher

All schools are private and fee-paying. This schoolmaster is holding a class in the house where he lives. He teaches reading, writing and mathematics.

### Theseus

Theseus was Athens' favourite hero. The most famous of his many adventures was slaying the Minotaur, a bull-headed monster that lived at the heart of a labyrinth (maze) on the island of Crete.

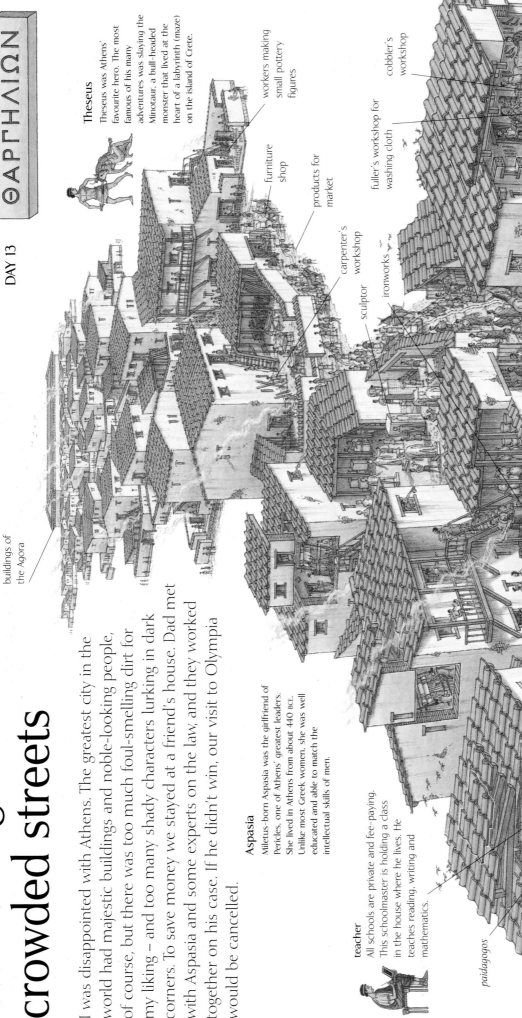

buildings of the Agora

workers making small pottery figures

furniture shop

products for market

carpenter's workshop

fuller's workshop for washing cloth

sculptor

ironworks

cobbler's workshop

paidagogos

jeweller's workshop

charcoal store

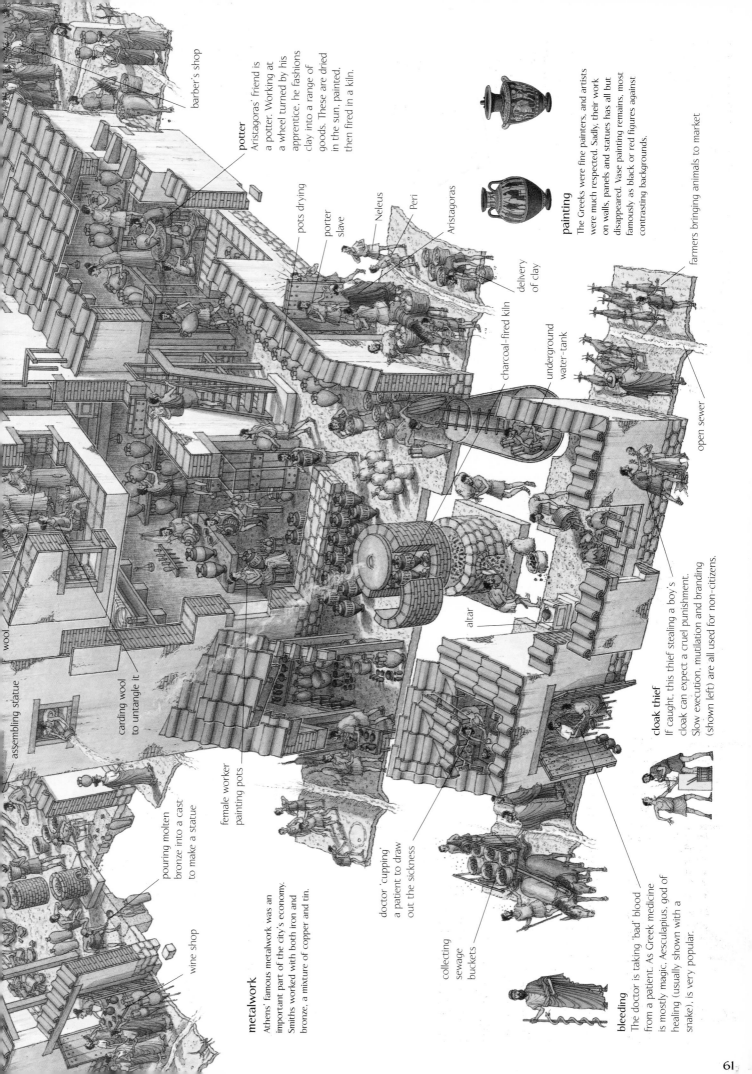

barber's shop

**potter**
Aristagoras' friend is a potter. Working at a wheel turned by his apprentice, he fashions clay into a range of goods. These are dried in the sun, painted, then fired in a kiln.

pots drying

porter slave

Neleus

Peri

Aristagoras

delivery of clay

**painting**
The Greeks were fine painters, and artists were much respected. Sadly, their work on walls, panels and statues has all but disappeared. Vase painting remains, most famously as black or red figures against contrasting backgrounds.

farmers bringing animals to market

charcoal-fired kiln

underground water-tank

open sewer

wool

assembling statue

carding wool to untangle it

altar

**metalwork**
Athens' famous metalwork was an important part of the city's economy. Smiths worked with both iron and bronze, a mixture of copper and tin.

pouring molten bronze into a cast to make a statue

female worker painting pots

doctor 'cupping' a patient to draw out the sickness

**cloak thief**
If caught, this thief stealing a boy's cloak can expect a cruel punishment. Slow execution, mutilation and branding (shown left) are all used for non-citizens.

wine shop

collecting sewage buckets

**bleeding**
The doctor is taking 'bad' blood from a patient. As Greek medicine is mostly magic, Aesculapius, god of healing (usually shown with a snake), is very popular.

61

# Shopping in the Agora

We explored the Agora while dad finally had his day in court. As I examined a figurine that I wanted to buy for mum, a cutpurse stole my money. Luckily, our *paidagogos* grabbed him and sent Peri off to fetch the Scythian police. At that moment dad turned up, waving his arms and grinning like Jason when he grabbed the Golden Fleece. He'd won! Lyrias was guilty and had to repay all the money. Our trip to Olympia was on!

### Pericles

Pericles (c. 495–429 BCE) was the greatest of all Athens' political leaders. While extending the city's power, he upheld the freedom of individual citizens and launched the building programme that was going on during the Milesians' visit.

### democracy

Athenian democracy was based on the idea that all citizens were equal and free. The assembly of citizens was the most powerful body in the state. Unlike most modern democracies, however, women were excluded.

### Bouleuterion

The day-to-day running of Athens is in the hands of a 500-strong council known as the Boule. The Boule meets in the Bouleuterion, mainly to decide what matters are to be discussed at the next citizens' assembly.

### Agora

Although all Greek cities had an agora, or market place, Athens' was the grandest. It was surrounded by fine public buildings in which much of the city's financial, political and religious business was carried on.

### Scythians

Scythians, from the region north of the Black Sea, are brilliant horsemen and archers. They are employed as Athens' professional police force.

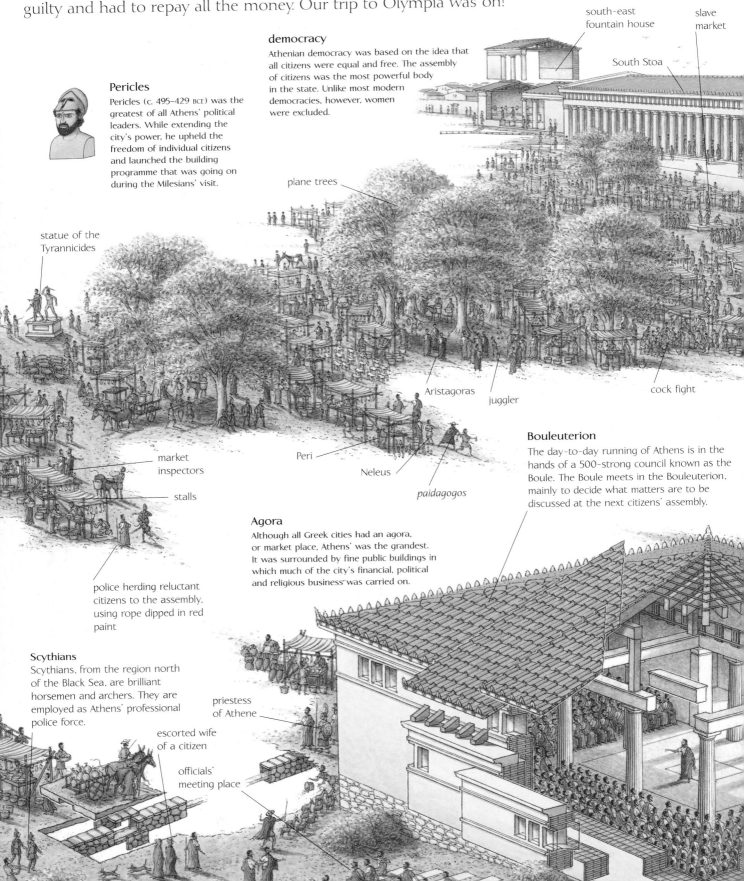

- south-east fountain house
- slave market
- South Stoa
- plane trees
- statue of the Tyrannicides
- Aristagoras
- juggler
- cock fight
- market inspectors
- Peri
- stalls
- Neleus
- *paidagogos*
- police herding reluctant citizens to the assembly, using rope dipped in red paint
- priestess of Athene
- escorted wife of a citizen
- officials' meeting place

## Hephaestus

Only in Athens was there a temple of the fire god Hephaestus. Supposedly lame, this ingenious son of Zeus and Hera was not popular elsewhere. The Athenians liked him because he watched over their many smiths.

## Aphrodite

According to legend, Aphrodite, the elegant goddess of beauty and love, was born out of sea foam. She became the wife of Hephaestus and the lover of Ares.

## Athenian law

When a citizen was charged with breaking Athens' carefully worded law, the case was argued before a jury of several hundred citizens. They reached their decision by a secret vote, using a hollow voting token to indicate a guilty verdict, a solid one if they felt the accused was innocent.

mud-brick walls

banking tables

dining rooms

Aristagoras' friend's house

jury

lawcourt

prosecutor and defendant

machine for jury selection

## Eponymous Heroes

These figures represent the heroes who gave their names to the 10 tribes of Attica, Athens' city-state.

## lawyers

Athens had no full-time lawyers. People hired experts to help write a speech that argued their side of the case. They delivered the speech themselves.

great drain

drain pipe

boundary stone

water clock for timing speeches

## Tholos

A committee of 50 citizens meet here to decide what will be discussed at public meetings.

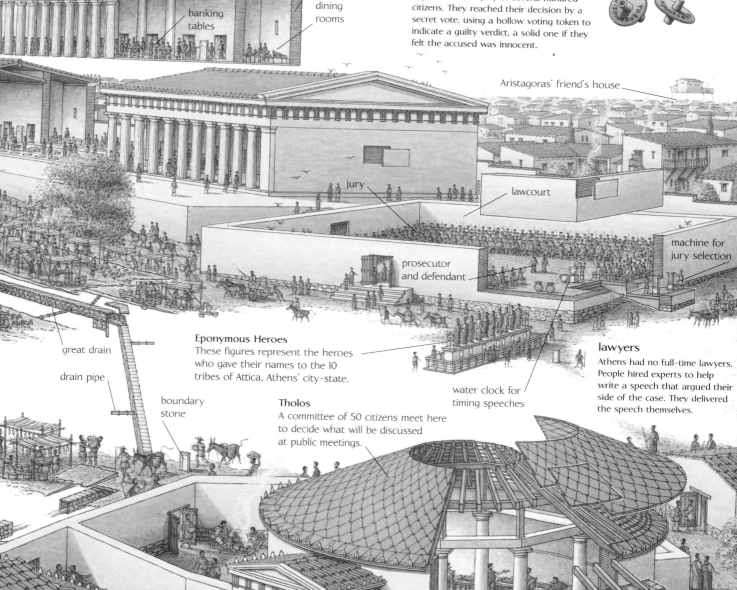

official weights and measures

market inspectors checking a roof tile

army officers

## ostracism

Once a year, Athenian citizens could vote to ostracize (send out of the country) one of their number for 10 years. Ostracism, not necessarily a disgrace, was a means of getting rid of powerful men who might threaten democracy. Votes were written on pieces of broken pottery (ostraka).

# The Acropolis and theatre of Dionysus

Dad's opinion of Athens had changed completely. He now loved the city and wanted to live there. Horrified, I begged him to check first with the oracle at Delphi. He agreed. Before we left, we climbed the Acropolis, gave thanks to Athene, and visited the theatre. Here the famous poet Sophocles was rehearsing his play *Ajax*. Guess who ruined the show? Wandering backstage in an actor's mask, Peri tripped and crashed noisily down some wooden steps.

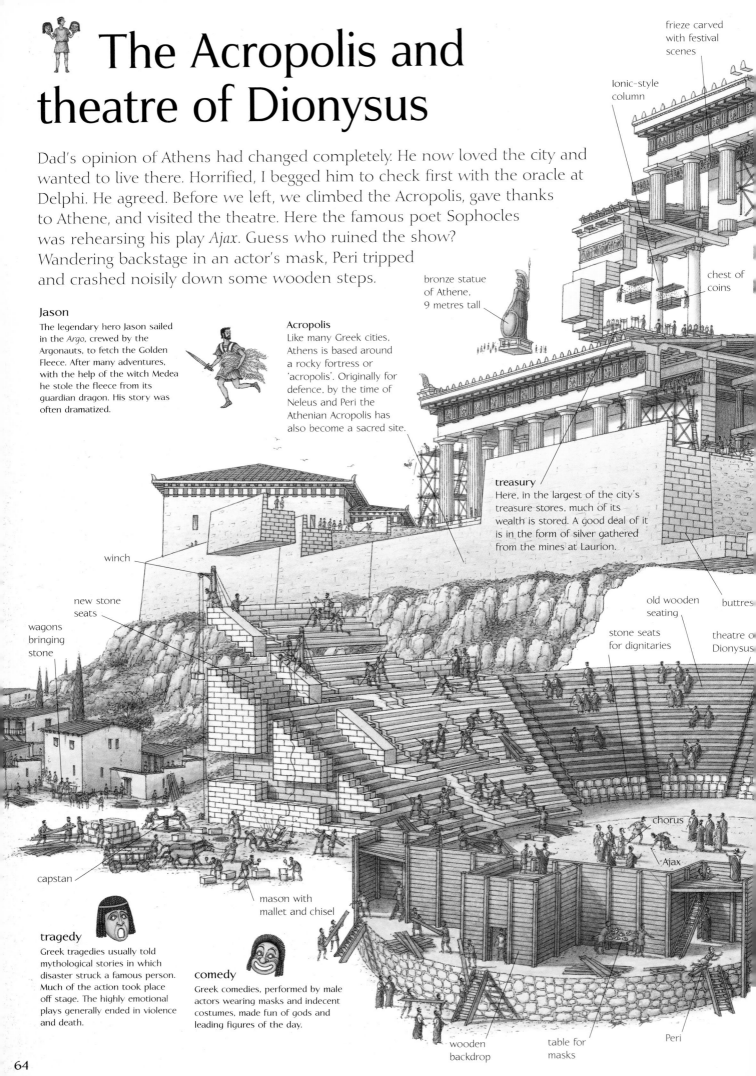

**frieze carved with festival scenes**

**Ionic-style column**

**chest of coins**

### Jason
The legendary hero Jason sailed in the *Argo*, crewed by the Argonauts, to fetch the Golden Fleece. After many adventures, with the help of the witch Medea he stole the fleece from its guardian dragon. His story was often dramatized.

### Acropolis
Like many Greek cities, Athens is based around a rocky fortress or 'acropolis'. Originally for defence, by the time of Neleus and Peri the Athenian Acropolis has also become a sacred site.

**bronze statue of Athene, 9 metres tall**

### treasury
Here, in the largest of the city's treasure stores, much of its wealth is stored. A good deal of it is in the form of silver gathered from the mines at Laurion.

**winch**

**new stone seats**

**wagons bringing stone**

**old wooden seating**

**buttres[s]**

**stone seats for dignitaries**

**theatre o[f] Dionysus**

**chorus**

**Ajax**

**capstan**

**mason with mallet and chisel**

**Peri**

### tragedy
Greek tragedies usually told mythological stories in which disaster struck a famous person. Much of the action took place off stage. The highly emotional plays generally ended in violence and death.

### comedy
Greek comedies, performed by male actors wearing masks and indecent costumes, made fun of gods and leading figures of the day.

**wooden backdrop**

**table for masks**

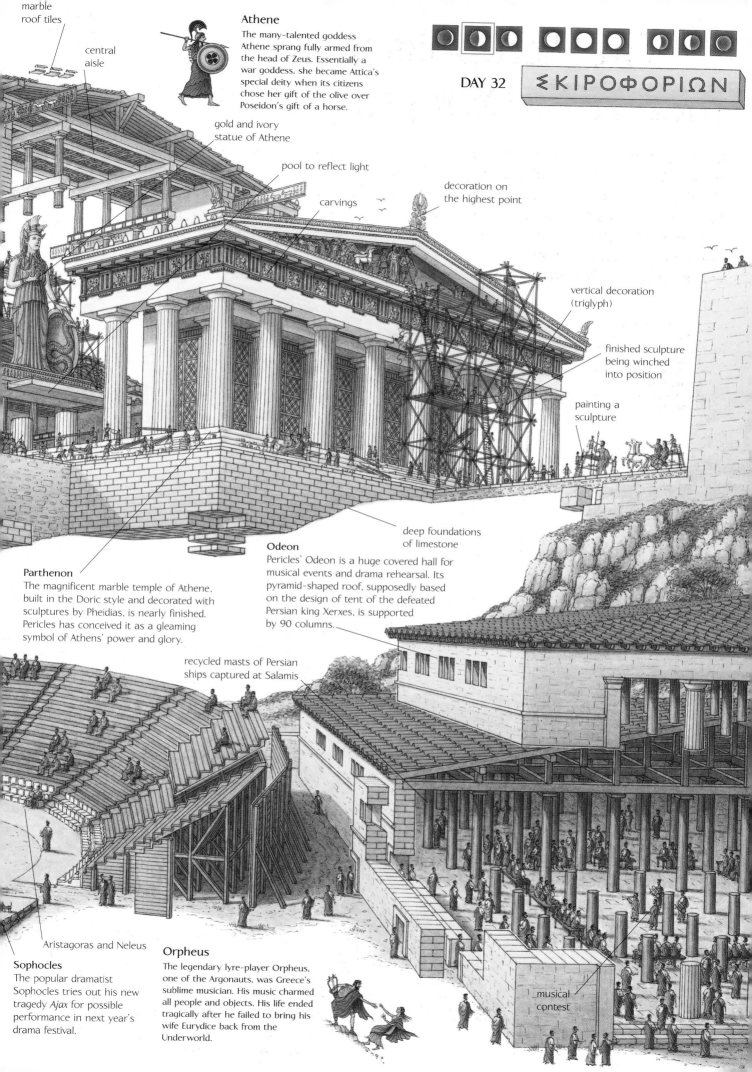

marble roof tiles

central aisle

## Athene
The many-talented goddess Athene sprang fully armed from the head of Zeus. Essentially a war goddess, she became Attica's special deity when its citizens chose her gift of the olive over Poseidon's gift of a horse.

gold and ivory statue of Athene

pool to reflect light

carvings

decoration on the highest point

vertical decoration (triglyph)

finished sculpture being winched into position

painting a sculpture

deep foundations of limestone

## Parthenon
The magnificent marble temple of Athene, built in the Doric style and decorated with sculptures by Pheidias, is nearly finished. Pericles has conceived it as a gleaming symbol of Athens' power and glory.

## Odeon
Pericles' Odeon is a huge covered hall for musical events and drama rehearsal. Its pyramid-shaped roof, supposedly based on the design of tent of the defeated Persian king Xerxes, is supported by 90 columns.

recycled masts of Persian ships captured at Salamis

## Sophocles
The popular dramatist Sophocles tries out his new tragedy *Ajax* for possible performance in next year's drama festival.

Aristagoras and Neleus

## Orpheus
The legendary lyre-player Orpheus, one of the Argonauts, was Greece's sublime musician. His music charmed all people and objects. His life ended tragically after he failed to bring his wife Eurydice back from the Underworld.

musical contest

# Apollo's temple at Delphi

We sailed to Delphi past the site of the Greeks' great naval victory at Salamis. The shrine of Apollo, the navel of the Earth, is an eerie place. Should we stay at Miletus, we asked the god, or move to Athens? I was shaking with fear when the priest brought the answer: 'Wisdom will appear at Olympia.' Dad said this meant if Boulos became Olympic wrestling champion, we'd stay in Miletus. If not, we'd move.

### sanctuary of Apollo

The sanctuary, close to where the god once performed heroic deeds, lay at the heart of one of Greece's most popular places of pilgrimage.

### oracles

The commonest way for men and gods to communicate was through an oracle. This was a shrine where a priest or priestess could contact the resident deity, usually to obtain an (ambiguous) answer to a question.

### dedications

Delphi's many statues, armour and other offerings were dedicated to Apollo in thanks for his assistance. This famous statue of a charioteer was a mark of gratitude for a chariot team's victory in the local games.

### Apollo

The beautiful young god Apollo, a perfect Greek male, was associated with reason, music, archery, medicine and, above all, prophesy. The island of Delos, where he and his sister Artemis were born, was sacred to him.

river god

deities

Leto, a female Titan, mother of Apollo

Apollo

the snake-monster Python

Gaia (Earth), mother of the Python

deities

sphinx

river god

Doric-style capital

gold-plated doors

waiting chamber

Apollo

eagle

ΣΚΙΡΟΦΟΡΙΩΝ

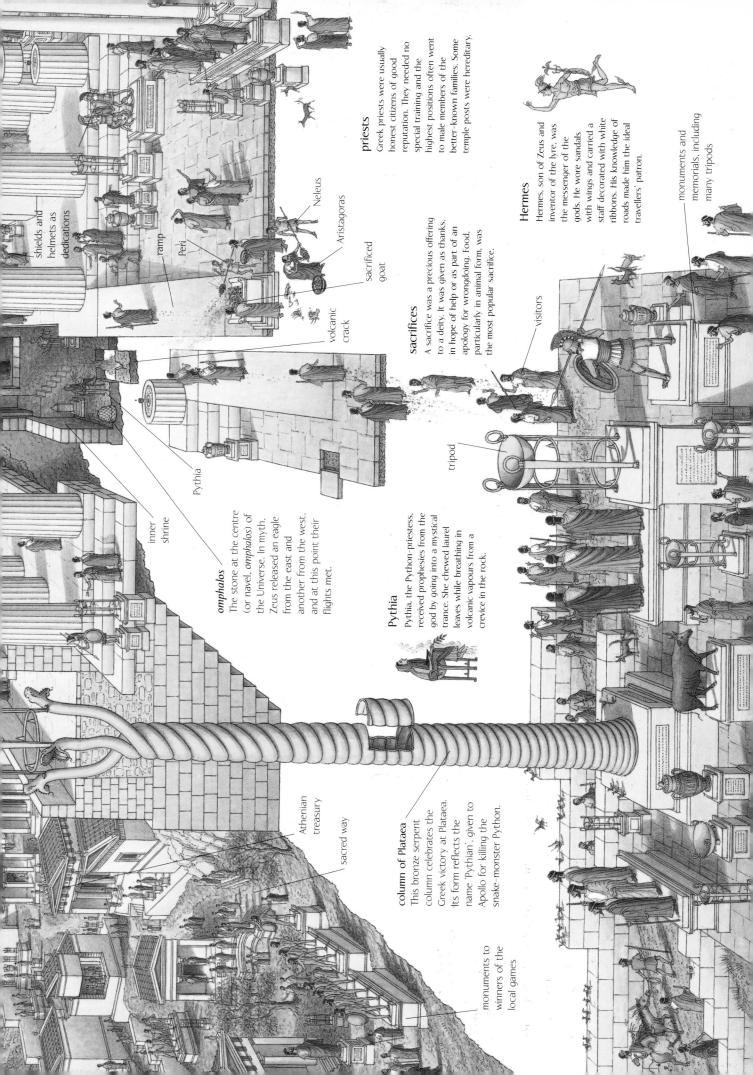

shields and helmets as dedications

ramp

Peri

Neleus

Aristagoras

sacrificed goat

volcanic crack

inner shrine

Pythia

omphalos

Athenian treasury

sacred way

monuments to winners of the local games

visitors

tripod

## priests

Greek priests were usually honest citizens of good reputation. They needed no special training and the highest positions often went to male members of the better-known families. Some temple posts were hereditary.

## Hermes

Hermes, son of Zeus and inventor of the lyre, was the messenger of the gods. He wore sandals with wings and carried a staff decorated with white ribbons. His knowledge of roads made him the ideal travellers' patron.

monuments and memorials, including many tripods

## sacrifices

A sacrifice was a precious offering to a deity. It was given as thanks, in hope of help or as part of an apology for wrongdoing. Food, particularly in animal form, was the most popular sacrifice.

## omphalos

The stone at the centre (or navel, *omphalos*) of the Universe. In myth, Zeus released an eagle from the east and another from the west, and at this point their flights met.

## Pythia

Pythia, the Python-priestess, received prophesies from the god by going into a mystical trance. She chewed laurel leaves while breathing in volcanic vapours from a crevice in the rock.

## column of Plataea

This bronze serpent column celebrates the Greek victory at Plataea. Its form reflects the name 'Pythian', given to Apollo for killing the snake-monster Python.

# The Olympic Games

Boulos' wrestling final was on the third day of the Games. His opponent was an Athenian, and a huge crowd gathered to watch. Peri and I climbed a tree to get a good view. Imagine our joy when, after a long fight, Boulos triumphed. We were staying in Miletus! Peri was so happy he fell out of the tree. He'll never be an athlete, just as I'll never be an Athenian.

## Olympic Games

After completing one of his legendary labours, Greece's most famous hero Heracles founded the Olympic Games in honour of his father Zeus. Staged every fourth summer from 776 BCE, they were open to all males from across the Greek world.

## Olympic Truce

The Olympic Truce was a one-month period (later three months) during which warfare and legal disputes between states were banned. This meant the Games were not disrupted by fighting, and competitors and visitors could attend in safety.

## Zeus

The position of Zeus as king of the gods was based upon sheer power. He became king by killing his Titan father, Kronos. He was father of five other deities as well as many other children by different mothers.

## the Altis

This walled part of the site, originally an olive grove, is sacred to Zeus. It contains the temples of Zeus and Hera, treasuries, and other religious structures.

## wrestling

This type of wrestling is won by throwing an opponent to the ground three times. In the more violent 'pankration' kicking, punching and strangling are allowed, but not biting or gouging.

hill of Kronos

Hera and Hermes

temple of Hera

paintings of women athletes

Boulos

judge

Aristagoras

Neleus

Peri

workshop of the sculptor Pheidias

winch

Pheidias

ivory-plated panel

gold and ivory statue of Zeus being built to replace the old image in the temple

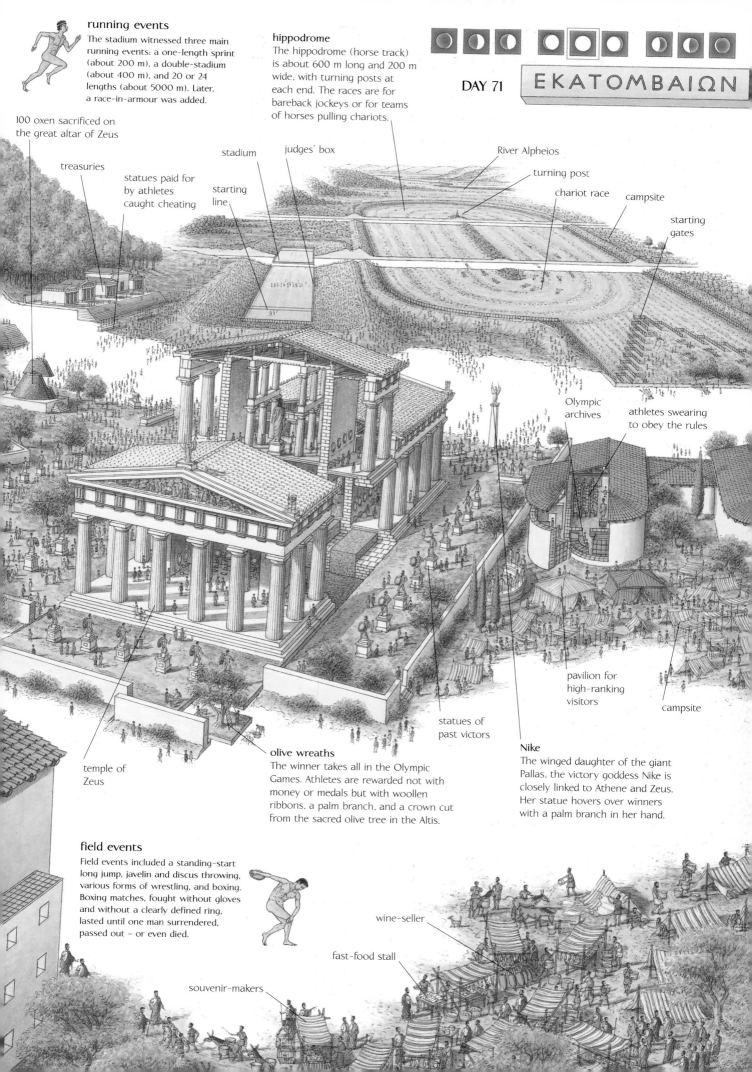

**running events**
The stadium witnessed three main running events: a one-length sprint (about 200 m), a double-stadium (about 400 m), and 20 or 24 lengths (about 5000 m). Later, a race-in-armour was added.

**hippodrome**
The hippodrome (horse track) is about 600 m long and 200 m wide, with turning posts at each end. The races are for bareback jockeys or for teams of horses pulling chariots.

100 oxen sacrificed on the great altar of Zeus

treasuries

statues paid for by athletes caught cheating

stadium

starting line

judges' box

River Alpheios

turning post

chariot race

campsite

starting gates

Olympic archives

athletes swearing to obey the rules

statues of past victors

pavilion for high-ranking visitors

campsite

temple of Zeus

**olive wreaths**
The winner takes all in the Olympic Games. Athletes are rewarded not with money or medals but with woollen ribbons, a palm branch, and a crown cut from the sacred olive tree in the Altis.

**Nike**
The winged daughter of the giant Pallas, the victory goddess Nike is closely linked to Athene and Zeus. Her statue hovers over winners with a palm branch in her hand.

**field events**
Field events included a standing-start long jump, javelin and discus throwing, various forms of wrestling, and boxing. Boxing matches, fought without gloves and without a clearly defined ring, lasted until one man surrendered, passed out – or even died.

wine-seller

fast-food stall

souvenir-makers

# Glossary

**acropolis:** a fortified and often sacred high point at the heart of a Greek city.

**Afterlife:** the Egyptians believed that death was just a transition between life on Earth and the Afterlife. Descriptions of the latter vary from people becoming stars to their continuing to live an Earth-style life in the fertile Field of Reeds.

**agora:** an open space in a Greek city for markets, meetings, games and so forth.

**Altar:** a flat-topped stone block where priests sacrificed animals to the gods.

**Amduat:** a text describing the nightly journey of the Sun through the Duat, the dark Underworld region beneath the Earth.

**Amphitheatre:** a round, open building with tiers of seats, where gladiator contests and wild animal hunts took place.

**Amphora:** a large, round-bottomed pottery jar, used for storing such things as olive oil, wine and fish sauce.

**Amulet:** a small charm with magic or holy power, often in the shape of a sacred animal or object. It was worn to protect its owner or to give them special strength.

**atrium:** a large hallway at the front of a Roman house. The roof of the atrium was open at the centre, and there was a pool to catch rainwater under the opening.

**Attica:** the name of the city-state of which Athens was the capital.

**Augustus:** the first Roman emperor. He ruled the empire for 41 years, from 27 bc to ad 14. Before Augustus, the empire was run by the Senate and the consuls.

**basilica:** a large building with an open space in the centre and colonnades (walkways lined with columns) along the sides. Basilicas were used for law courts and as places for holding large meetings.

**Bint-Anath** (died around 1213 BCE) was Egyptian pharaoh Rameses II's eldest daughter, who later became his favourite queen.

**Book of Gates:** a text in Egyptian guiding a deceased person through the complex network of doors and passageways of the Underworld to the chamber where they would be judged.

**Book of the Dead:** an Egyptian collection of up to 190 spells, often written on papyrus and placed inside a coffin, to assist a deceased person in their quest to enter the Afterlife.

**branding:** deliberately marking the skin with a red-hot iron.

**bronze:** a tough mixture of tin and copper.

**caldarium:** the hot room of the Roman baths.

**canopic jar:** one of a set of four jars, stored within a canopic chest, in which were kept the preserved internal organs of a mummified body (except the heart and kidneys, which remained with the body) in Egypt.

**cataract:** rocky rapids that make a river impassable to boats.

**cesspit:** a deep hole used for rubbish and sewage.

**Circus Maximus:** the largest chariot-racing arena in Rome. All chariot race-tracks were called circuses, and maximus means 'biggest'.

**clients:** poorer citizens, who relied on someone rich and powerful (their patron) for work and protection. In return, the clients helped the patron and did jobs for him, especially at election times.

**Colosseum:** the largest amphitheatre in Rome, where emperors held gladiatorial games.

**consuls:** the two top Roman officials. In the time of the emperors, one of the consuls was often the emperor. The consuls were elected every year.

**corselet:** a close-fitting, sleeveless leather jacket worn to protect the body.

**Curia:** the building at the centre of Rome where the emperor and the senators (Rome's richest and most powerful people) met to discuss the running of the empire.

**democracy:** government by the citizens, first introduced in Greece.

**Djoser** (2667–2648 BCE) was the Egyptian king for whom the Step Pyramid at Saqqara was built.

**Domitian:** emperor of Rome from ad 81 to 96.

**Doric:** a simple and solid style of architecture.

**elections:** events where people voted to choose who would be the consuls, judges and other officials in charge of running the empire.

**equites:** Romans who were wealthy, but not as well-off as senators. Many of them were involved in running the empire or had quite important jobs in the army.

**forum:** a public square or market-place. There were many forums in Rome and in the many towns and cities of the empire. The most important one was the Forum Romanum (Roman Forum) in the centre of Rome.

**freedman or freedwoman:** a man or woman who had been a slave but was now free. Slaves were freed by their masters if they served them well for a long time. Slaves could also buy their freedom, if they could earn enough money to do so.

**frieze:** a decorated stone band above the columns of a building.

**frigidarium:** the cold room of the Roman baths.

**garum:** see liquamen.

**gladiator:** someone who fought in the Roman amphitheatre to entertain people. Most gladiators were prisoners of war or criminals. They were forced to fight, often to the death. However, a successful gladiator could become rich and famous.

**Hades:** see Underworld.

**Hadrian:** emperor of Rome from ad 117 to 138, including the time of our story.

**Hatshepsut** (1473–1458 BCE) was perhaps the most successful of all the women who ruled as pharaohs.

**hieroglyphs:** Ancient Egypt's complex system of writing used three types of hieroglyphic symbol. Some were diagrams of the thing they represented, others represented sounds or ideas. Modern scholars could not read hieroglyphic writing until the discovery in 1799 and deciphering in 1822 of the Rosetta stone – an artefact inscribed with the same text in three languages, including hieroglyphs and the familiar ancient Greek.

**Homer:** a semi-legendary Greek poet who supposedly wrote the epic poems the *Iliad* (about the fall of Troy) and the *Odyssey* (about the travels of the hero Odysseus).

**hoplite:** a heavily armoured Greek foot soldier equipped with a shield, sword and spear.

**hoplomachus:** the most common heavily armed Roman gladiator. The hoplomachus carried a large rectangular shield and a straight sword.

**hypocaust:** underfloor central heating. This type of heating was widely used in Roman public buildings and larger houses.

**hypostyle:** a court filled with many pillars. These represented reeds growing around the mound from which the Earth had been made at the time of creation.

**impluvium:** the pool below the opening in the atrium roof, where rainwater collected.

**incense:** a substance that gives off a sweet or spicy smell when it is burnt. Incense was burnt in Roman temples, especially during religious ceremonies.

**Inundation:** the annual flooding of the Nile's banks as waters rushed down from the African highlands to the south. The Egyptians gave great religious significance to this seemingly miraculous event that brought life to an otherwise barren desert.

**Ionia:** a region that extends along the west coast of modern-day Turkey.

**Ionic:** a style of architecture featuring scroll-like decoration at the top of columns.

**Ka:** In Egypt, a person's life force – the key difference between them and an individual who had died. As long as it was fed and cherished, the Ka might live on after earthly death. When this happened, it also protected and nourished the deceased person's body.

**Khafra** (2558–2532 BCE), whose face is supposed to be on the Great Sphinx of Giza, was the son of Khufu.

**Khufu** (2589–2566 BCE) was the king who built the Great Pyramid of Giza.

**lararium:** the shrine (worshipping place) of the Roman household gods.

**liquamen** (garum): a very spicy fish sauce, widely used by Romans in their cooking.

**Ludus Magnus:** the largest training school for gladiators in Rome. A tunnel connected it to the Colosseum.

**lyre:** a musical instrument like a hand-held harp.

**Mars:** the Roman god of war.

**mastaba:** a solid-looking low tomb with outward-sloping walls. Some of the earliest Egyptian royal burials were made beneath these bench-shaped structures.

**metic:** a resident foreigner.

**mosaic:** a covering for a floor or wall, made from many coloured pieces of glass or stone fitted together to make a picture or pattern.

**natron:** a compound of sodium that occurred in and around the sites of Egypt's prehistoric lakes. It was used for all kinds of cleaning purposes, most famously for drying out a corpse for mummification.

**nave:** the central part of a Roman basilica. The name later came to be used for the central part of a church.

**Nilometer:** a device, often consisting of simple steps leading down to the water, by which the level of the River Nile was measured. It is not clear why this information was needed, but it seems to have been for religious, taxation or agricultural purposes.

**obelisk:** a needle-shaped stone monument connected to Sun worship. Baboons, famous for getting excited at sunrise, were often carved around the foot of an obelisk in Egypt.

**oracle:** a place in Greece where people consulted a deity who was supposed to foretell the future.

**ocella:** a Roman snack, consisting of a flat round of bread topped with olives and cheese. It was similar to a modern pizza, but had no tomatoes (tomatoes were not grown in Europe in Roman times).

**osculum:** a disc made of metal or other shiny substances that was hung up in such a way as to flash when it caught the light.

**Ostia:** the main port for Rome. Rome is on the Tiber river, but large boats could not sail up the river because it was too shallow. They had to unload at the coast, at Ostia.

**paidagogos:** a slave appointed to supervise children.

**papyrus:** a large, dense reed that grew beside the Nile and had many uses. It was woven into baskets and boats, and hammered into an early form of paper.

**patron:** a protector and helper.

**pharaoh:** often used rather inaccurately to refer to any Egyptian ruler, pharaoh originally meant the royal palace ('per-aa' or 'great house'). By the middle of the 2nd millennium BCE, it was being used for the monarch (male or female) who occupied that house.

**philosopher:** a 'lover of wisdom' and seeker after truth in all things.

**pigment:** natural colouring which was mixed with oil or water to make paint or ink.

**portico:** a flat roof, supported by pillars, that forms a porch to a building. Porticoes were built on apartment buildings in Rome to help firefighters reach the upper floors in a fire.

**Praetorian Guard:** the soldiers of the emperor's personal bodyguard.

**pylon:** a huge, highly decorated gateway representing the pillars of the horizon through which the Sun rose each day. It comprised two tapering towers linked by a lower bridge-type construction.

**pyramidion:** a single pyramid-shaped stone placed at the top of a pyramid or obelisk. Many were gilded – covered in a thin layer of gold that shone in the rays of the Sun.

**quadriga:** a four-horse chariot.

**Rameses II** (1279–1213 BCE) ruled for many years and built or took over a vast number of monuments, earning himself the title 'Rameses the Great'.

**retiarius:** a lightly-armed gladiator. A retiarius had no shield, but carried a trident and a net.

**Rostra:** a platform in the Roman Forum where important speeches were made.

**sacrifice:** an animal, such as a goat or an ox, that was sacrificed (killed) as part of a religious ceremony.

**sarcophagus:** a container, usually of stone, in which one or more coffins were stored for protection. The Egyptian sarcophagus was normally carved and sometimes painted.

**scribe:** a respected professional writer who had mastered the complicated system of hieroglyphic writing.

**secutor:** a type of Roman gladiator. The secutor was heavily armed, with a helmet, sword and shield. His helmet was smooth, to avoid getting caught in the net of a retiarius.

**Senate House:** the meeting place for the Roman Senate, the group of rich, powerful politicians who, along with the emperor, ran the empire.

**senator:** a member of the Senate.

**senet:** a popular Egyptian game in which each player had seven pieces on a board of 30 squares in three rows of 10. Moves were determined by chance, and the object seems to have been to guide one's pieces along a twisting path – a bit like a sophisticated kind of snakes and ladders.

**serdab:** a room in a mastaba tomb where a statue of the deceased's Ka was usually placed. The chamber wall had one or more small openings for offerings to be passed in and through which the Ka could venture out.

**Sette Sale:** a reservoir where water for the Baths of Trajan was stored.

**shaduf:** a device for lifting water that has been in use for thousands of years. The scoop on one end of a hinged pole is counterbalanced by a weight on the other.

**shrine:** a holy place for the worship and honouring of a deity.

**sphinx:** a creature with the head of a human or other animal, and the body of a lion. It was associated with the king and Sun worship.

**spina:** the 'central reservation' running down the middle of the Circus Maximus.

**stela:** a stone or wood slab on which paintings, carvings or writings were displayed. They were often associated with caring for the dead.

**strigil:** a scraper, used to scrape oil from the skin. Romans did not wash: instead they oiled themselves and then scraped off the dirty oil to get clean.

**stoa:** an open building, with a roof supported by columns, used for meetings.

**symposium:** an all-male drinking party.

**Tarquin** was the fourth of Rome's seven kings. He ruled from 616 to 579 bc.

**tepidarium:** the warm room of the Roman baths.

**Thutmose III** (1479–1425 BCE), a successful warrior king, was buried in the Valley of the Kings.

**Titans:** in Greek mythology, the first creatures on the Earth, who were defeated and replaced by the gods.

**toga:** a garment worn by Roman men, which consisted of a large piece of woollen cloth draped about the body.

**Trajan:** emperor of Rome from ad 98 to 117.

**treasury:** a place where money and valuable objects were stored, for future use or as gifts to a deity.

**tribute:** payment made to a conquering power. When its empire was at its furthest extent, tribute poured into Egypt from all around the Near East. Although in theory semi-voluntary, it was really a type of tax.

**trident:** a large three-pronged fork for fishing or fighting.

**tripod:** a three-footed support for vessels.

**trireme:** a warship with three banks of oars.

**tunic:** a piece of clothing, consisting of a rectangle of cloth with a hole for the head, held by a belt at the waist.

**Two Crowns:** Egypt was once two kingdoms, Upper Egypt (south), represented by a white crown, and Lower Egypt (north), represented by a red crown. After the two were united around 3000 BCE, rulers could wear the double crown of Upper and Lower Egypt. The country itself was sometimes referred to as the 'Land of the Two Crowns'.

**Unas** (2375–2345 BCE) was buried close to the Saqqara Step Pyramid.

**Underworld:** known as the Duat in Egypt and Hades in Roman and Greek, the Underworld was the dark region beneath the Earth through which the Sun sailed each night in a boat.

**vault:** an arched ceiling. Vaulted roofs can span larger distances between supports than a flat roof can.

**venatores:** wild animal hunters, part of the entertainment at the amphitheatre.

**vomitoria:** entrances and exits in the Colosseum seating area.

# Gods and Goddesses

(Note: Names in brackets denote Roman name)

### Amun-Ra

Amun, whose name may mean 'the hidden one', was a popular god of the Thebes region who became known as the 'king of the gods'. Sometimes shown with a ram's head, he was commonly linked to another popular and powerful deity, the Sun god Ra.

### Anubis

The Egyptian jackal-headed Anubis was god of the dead and guardian of cemeteries. Connected with mummification, his black colour was a reminder of the fertile soil found on the banks of the Nile.

### Aphrodite (Venus)

One legend says that Aphrodite, the elegant goddess of beauty and love, was born out of sea foam. Other sources say she was a child of Zeus. She became wife of Hephaestus, lover of Ares, and mother of Eros.

### Apollo (Apollo)

The beautiful young god Apollo, a perfect Greek male, was associated with reason, music, archery, medicine, and above all prophesy, especially at the Delphic oracle. The island of Delos, where he and his twin sister Artemis were born, was sacred to him.

### Ares (Mars)

Ares, the bloody, merciless yet sometimes cowardly god of war, was hated by his parents, Zeus and Hera. He had only one admirer, Hades, ruler of the Underworld, because Ares' antics helped populate his kingdom of dead souls.

### Artemis (Diana)

The virgin deity Artemis was the goddess of hunting, animals and childbirth. She was also associated with the Moon. Her temple at Ephesus was one of the Seven Wonders of the ancient world.

### Athene (Minerva)

Many-talented Athene, goddess of war and patron of arts and crafts, was wisdom in god-like form. She became Attica's special deity because when she offered its people the olive, they chose it over Poseidon's gift of a horse.

### Atum

An ancient Egyptian creator god, Atum was also worshipped as a Sun god. Like Amun, he became closely linked with Ra, another Sun god.

### Castor and Pollux

Twin Roman gods, the gods of horsemen, sailors, and of friendship. Castor was a horse-tamer, Pollux a boxer.

### Demeter (Ceres)

The mystical goddess of corn and all fruits of the Earth, Demeter was also closely linked to the Underworld:her daughter Persephone was married to the grim lord Hades. Rituals in honour of Demeter focused on death and rebirth.

### Dionysus (Bacchus)

The god of wine and wild parties was usually accompanied by leaping satyrs (woodland spirits). Athens' leading drama festival, the spring Dionysia, was held in his honour. Some of the festivities associated with him were very wild and unrestrained.

### Geb

A green-coloured god of the Earth, Geb, like Osiris, was responsible for vegetation in Egypt.

### Hephaestus (Vulcan)

Hephaestus, son of Zeus and Hera, was the ingenious god of fire and metal-workers. His forge was under the volcanic Mount Etna. Athens, seeking protection for its many smiths, was the only city to honour him with a temple.

### Hera (Juno)

The sister-wife of Zeus and queen of the gods, Hera was the guardian of women, the home and children. She could be cruel, though, particularly towards her husband's innumerable girlfriends.

### Hermes (Mercury)

Hermes, son of Zeus and inventor of the lyre, was the messenger of the gods. He wore sandals with wings and carried a staff decorated with white ribbons. His knowledge of roads made him the ideal travellers' patron.

### Horus

The ancient falcon god Horus was a sky god and one of the protectors of Egypt's reigning king. Indeed, he was kingship itself in living form. His parents were the famous brother and sister lovers, Isis and Osiris.

### Khnum

The ram god of Elephantine was linked to the Inundation, creativity and pottery.

### Mut

Mut was the partner of Amun and holy mother of the ruling king in Egypt. One of the daughters of the Sun, she was shown brightly clothed with a vulture head-dress.

### Nut

Nut was the Egyptian sky goddess whose body arched like the sky overhead. Some traditions said she swallowed the setting Sun every evening and gave birth to it again each morning. She was the sister-wife of the Earth god Geb.

### Osiris

One of the earliest and most important Egyptian gods, Osiris was commonly shown as a royal mummy. He was associated with death, rebirth and fertility, and was commonly coloured green (vegetation) or black (soil). As the brother-partner of Isis, he fathered the falcon god Horus.

### Poseidon (Neptune)

The mighty Poseidon ruled the kingdom of the seas. He was one of Zeus' brothers and was usually shown carrying a trident. The Athenians held him in double respect because of their seafaring traditions and because he was supposedly the father of their local hero Theseus.

### Venus

Roman goddess of love.

### Zeus (Jupiter)

Zeus was king of the gods. His authority was based upon sheer power – he became king, for example, by killing his Titan father, Kronos. Zeus was father of five Olympians and had many other children by different mothers. His name means 'sky'.

# Index

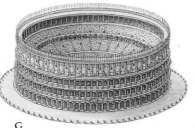

liquamen 46, 71
litter 37, 46
looms 17
Lower Egypt 8
Ludus Magnus 29, 39, 71
Luxor see Karnak
lyre 53, 71

## M

Maat 19
magic 8, 15
magistrates 28
Marathon 49, 51
marble 34, 36
market inspectors 62, 63
Mars 35, 73
masks 64
mastabas 21, 71
Mauretania 41
medicine 61
Mediterranean Sea 7
Memphis 7, 20
menageries 25
merchants 40-1
metals 8, 11
metalwork 61
Miletus 49, 51, 52–53
mine slaves 56
Minerva 34, 35, 73
mines 11, 37
Minotaur 60
Monte Testaccio 29, 40
Montu 13
mortuary temples 20
mosaics 30, 47, 71
mud-brick 11, 12, 16, 18, 22
mummies 14, 18–19
music and singing 8, 24, 25, 35, 47
musicians 53, 65
Mut 13, 73

## N

natron 11, 18, 71
nave 37, 71
Naxos 51
nightwatchmen 46
Nike 27
Nile (river) 5, 6–7, 22–23
Nile Delta 7
Nile Valley 6
Nilometer 9, 71
numbers 7
Nut 5, 15, 73

## O

obelisks 8, 12, 45, 71
ocella 33, 71
Odeon 65
Odysseus 50
oil lamps 15, 56
olive oil 29, 36, 40, 41, 42, 56
olive trees 56, 65, 27
Olympia 50
Olympic Games 68
Olympus, Mount 49, 50
oracles 66, 71
Orpheus 65
osculum 47, 71
Osiris 14, 19, 73
Ostia 40, 71
ostracism 63
owl (Athenian symbol) 54, 58

## P

paintings 14–15, 16, 18, 19, 24, 61
palaces 24–25
Palatine Hill 29
papyrus 8, 12, 13, 19, 23, 40, 71
Parthenon 50, 64–65
perfume 40, 41
Pericles 52, 60, 62, 65
Persephone 59
Persians 49, 55, 65, 67
pets 30
pharaohs 24, 45, 71
Pheidias 65, 68
philosophy 53
pigments 14, 71
Piraeus 51, 57, 58–59
Piramesse 7, 20, 24–25

plague 59
plaster 15, 18, 24
Plataea 49, 67
Plato 53
plays 64
ploughing 22
plumb lines 22

police 14, 62
politicians 28
porters 40-1
Poseidon 51, 54, 65, 73
potters 61
pottery 8, 9, 16, 17, 29, 33, 40, 41
Praetorian Guard 29, 71
priests 12, 13, 18, 19, 25, 34, 35, 67
prima mensa 47
prisoners 29, 37, 38
prisoners of war 9, 8
prophesy 66
pulvinar 45
punishment 61
pylons 12–13, 72
pyramidion 18, 72
pyramids 11, 20–21, 23
Pythagoras 51
Pythia 67

## Q

quadriga 44, 72
quarries 6, 8–11
Quirinal Hill 28

## R

Ra 13, 15
Rameses II 5, 9, 13, 14, 24–25
ramming 55
rats 59
relief carvings 15, 20
religion 5, 12–15, 16, 18–19, 20, 28, 31, 34–35
retiarius 38, 72
Rome 28-9
Rostra 28, 37, 28
rowing 8–9, 54–55
running events 27
rushes and reeds 8, 12, 16, 23, 25

## S

sacrifices 34, 35, 67, 72
sails 9, 8
Salamis 6, 51, 65, 66
salt 11
Sappho 51
Saqqara 7, 20–21
sarcophagi 15, 18, 21, 72
satyrs 53
science 53
scribes 6, 8, 11, 12, 25, 72
sculpture 60, 65
seafaring 54
seasons 7
secunda mensa 47
secutor 38, 72
Sed festival 21
Senate House 28, 36, 72
senators 28, 36, 37, 72
senet 17, 72
serdab 21, 72
Sette Sale 43, 72
settlements 55
shaduf 23, 72
ship-building 59
ships and boats 8–9, 8, 20, 22–23, 54–55
shops 28, 30, 33, 36, 37, 46
shrines 12, 16, 18, 28, 31, 36
silk 39, 41
silver mines 51, 56–57, 64
slaves and slavery 8–11, 29, 30, 31, 32, 37, 38, 41, 42, 47, 56, 62
Sobek 8
Socrates 53
Sophocles 64, 65
Spain 40, 41
Sparta 49, 51
sphinxes 13, 22–23, 72
spina 44, 72
spinning 53, 61
stadium 27
statues 13, 15, 34, 61
stelae 18, 72
Step Pyramid 7, 20–21
stepping stones 33
stone 8–11, 13, 17, 18, 23, 38–39, 40
streets 32–33, 46

strigil 42, 72
sundial 29
symposium 52
Syria 40, 41

## T

Tarquin 72
Taweret 8
taxes 9
teachers 60
temple of Apollo 66–67
temple of Athene see Parthenon
Temple of Castor and Pollux 37
Temple of Divus Julius 37
Temple of Faith 35
temple of Hera 68
Temple of Jupiter 28, 30, 34–35
Temple of Vesta 37
temple of Zeus 27
temples 6, 9, 11, 12–13, 20
tepidarium 42, 43, 72
theatre of Dionysus 50, 64
Theatre of Marcellus 28
Thebes 6
Thermopylae 49, 50
Theseus 54, 60
thieves 61
Tholos 63
Thracian 38
throwing sticks 22
Tiber, River 28, 40–1, 42
tiles 24
time 29
Titans 66, 68, 72
toga 72
toilets 9, 17, 31, 33
tombs 6, 14–15, 17–21
tools 8
torchbearers 46
toys and games 16, 53
trade 8–9, 36, 40–1, 54, 57
tragedy 64
Trajan 28, 72
transport 8–9, 14, 19, 20–21, 29, 32, 40–1, 46
treadmill 41
treasuries 64, 67, 27, 72
tribute 25, 54, 57, 72

triremes 50, 54–55, 58, 59
Troy 51
tunic 72
Two Crowns 6, 72

## U

Underworld (Duat) 14, 15, 55, 59, 65, 72

## V

Valley of the Kings 6, 14–15
Valley of the Queens 6
vases 61
vaulting 40, 42, 72
Velabrum 36
velaria 39
venatores 38, 72
Venus 35, 73
Venus Cloacina 36
Vesta 37
villages 16–17, 23
Viminal Hill 28
vomitoria 38, 72

## W

warehousing 29, 40–1
warships see triremes
washing 16, 42–3
water supply 29, 30, 32, 33, 43
weaving 8, 17, 23, 53
weights and measures 37
wet nurse 46
wheat 33, 40, 41
wheat 8, 8, 16, 17, 22
wigs 17
windows 12, 16
wine 29, 40, 41, 47, 52, 53, 61
women 17, 52, 59, 62
wood 11, 16, 18, 24, 40, 41, 55
wool 40, 41
wrestling 68
writing 7, 12, 14, 15, 18

## X

Xerxes 50, 65

## Z

Zeus 49, 50, 67, 68–27, 73

# Stephen Biesty

Stephen Biesty, the 'undisputed master of cutaway illustrations', is the creator of the million-copy bestselling Incredible Cross-sections series. His marvellous attention to detail results in spectacular illustrations that are as authoritative as they are beautiful.

# Stewart Ross

Stewart Ross, who wrote the Egypt and Greece sections of this book, is an award-winning historical writer, and one of Britain's most popular and versatile, with over 190 titles to his credit.

# Andrew Solway

Andrew Solway, who wrote the Rome section, is an experienced author and editor of children's books. Among his previous publications are *Ancient Rome* and *Ancient Greece*, both published by OUP.

## The Ancient World – general websites

**About.com: Ancient/Classical History**
http://ancienthistory.about.com/?once=true&

**Internet Ancient History Sourcebook**
http://www.fordham.edu/halsall/ancient/asbook.html

**Encyclopedia Mythica**
http://www.pantheon.org/

**BBC Ancient History**
http://www.bbc.co.uk/history/ancient/

### Rome

**LacusCurtius: A Gateway to Ancient Rome**
http://penelope.uchicago.edu/Thayer/E/Roman/home.html

**Capitolium: Official Website of the Imperial Forums**
http://www.capitolium.org/

### Egypt

**Egyptology Resources**
http://www.newton.cam.ac.uk/egypt/

**Eternal Egypt**
http://www.eternalegypt.org/EternalEgyptWebsiteWeb/HomeServlet

### Greece

**The Ancient Greek World**
http://www.museum.upenn.edu/Greek_World/Index.html

**Ancient Greece – The British Museum**
http://www.ancientgreece.co.uk/

## The Greek alphabet

The Greek alphabet, based on the Phoenician alphabet with the addition of vowels, appeared in the 8th century BCE. Our word 'alphabet' comes from its first two letters, alpha and beta. Here are the ancient Greek capital letters, with their names and English equivalents:

| A | alpha | a |
|---|---|---|
| B | beta | b |
| Γ | gamma | g |
| Δ | delta | d |
| E | epsilon | short e |
| Z | zeta | z |
| H | eta | long e |
| Θ | theta | th |
| I | iota | i |
| K | kappa | k |
| Λ | lambda | l |
| M | mu | m |
| N | nu | n |
| Ξ | xi | x |
| O | omicron | short o |
| Π | pi | p |
| P | rho | r |
| Σ | sigma | s |
| T | tau | t |
| Y | upsilon | u |
| Φ | phi | ph |
| X | chi | ch |
| Ψ | psi | psi |
| Ω | omega | long o |

# OXFORD
## UNIVERSITY PRESS

Great Clarendon Street, Oxford OX2 6DP

Oxford University Press is a department of the University of Oxford.
It furthers the University's objective of excellence in research, scholarship,
and education by publishing worldwide in

Oxford   New York

Auckland   Cape Town   Dar es Salaam   Hong Kong   Karachi
Kuala Lumpur   Madrid   Melbourne   Mexico City   Nairobi
New Delhi   Shanghai   Taipei   Toronto

With offices in

Argentina   Austria   Brazil   Chile   Czech Republic   France   Greece
Guatemala   Hungary   Italy   Japan   Poland   Portugal   Singapore
South Korea   Switzerland   Thailand   Turkey   Ukraine   Vietnam

Oxford is a registered trade mark of Oxford University Press
in the UK and in certain other countries

British Library Cataloguing in Publication Data

Data available

ISBN: 978-0-19-910965-4


1  3  5  7  9  10  8  6  4  2

Printed in Singapore